This book is published to accompany the television series entitled
Strictly Come Dancing, first broadcast on BBC1 in 2010.

Executive Producer: Moira Ross
Series Producers: Liz Trott and Ed Booth

BBC Books would like to thank Moira Ross, Liz Trott, Ed Booth, Jane Ashford, Claire Bridgland, Martin Scott, Richard Curwen, Leah Henry, Jagdeep Sharma, Richard Halliwell, Harriet Frost and the rest of the *Strictly Come Dancing* production team.

10 9 8 7 6 5 4 3 2 1

Published in 2010 by BBC Books, an imprint of Ebury Publishing.
A Random House Group Company

The Random House Group Limited Reg. No. 954009

Addresses for companies within the Random House Group can be found at
www.randomhouse.co.uk

A CIP catalogue record for this book is available from the British Library.

ISBN 978 1 849 90124 6

The Random House Group Limited supports the Forest Stewardship Council (FSC), the leading international forest certification organisation. All our titles that are printed on Greenpeace approved FSC certified paper carry the FSC logo. Our paper procurement policy can be found at
www.rbooks.co.uk/environment

Commissioning editor: Lorna Russell
Project editor: Laura Higginson
Copy-editor: Justine Taylor
Designer: Bobby Birchall, Bobby&Co
Production: Antony Heller

Series 7 photography by Guy Levy and Lee Strickland © BBC 2010; Series 8 photography by John Wright © BBC 2010; page 42t photography © Kabik/Retna Ltd./Corbis; pages 42b-45 © ABC Inc/Everett/Rex Features; pages 56-57 photography by Alex Thompson © BBC 2010; pages 58-61 photography © Alfie Hitchcock 2010; pages 82 and 94 by David Venni © BBC 2010.
All other photography © Fotolia.com
Colour origination by Altaimage, London
Printed and bound in Germany by Mohn Media GmbH

To buy books by your favourite authors and register for offers, visit www.rbooks.co.uk

The Official 2011 Annual

CONTENTS

A WORD FROM Bruce

Last year saw another fabulous series and another nailbiting final, this time between Chris Hollins and Ricky Whittle.

Ricky was so good, he could become a professional. In fact, by the end of the series he *was* a professional, as far as we were concerned. He had lovely lines and a lovely knack with the dance. He was a bit pigeon-toed at the beginning but anything he was told, he corrected straightaway, which was wonderful. The way some of the contestants just convert themselves into ballroom dancers is quite astounding.

Looking back, however, I don't think we've ever had another couple more popular than Chris and Ola. The rapport they had was amazing so they became a fantastic team to watch in their rehearsals and in their performances. They got on so well, and had the same sense of humour, which came over to the public. Whenever I announced them I could feel the excitement in the audience, because Chris and Ola meant it was going to be fun.

When the couples are thrown together, as they are, for four months, it's quite an ordeal in many cases, I would imagine, but they just got on from the word go. It was a perfect partnership. I played golf with Chris a few weeks ago at the BMW pro-am and he is a really good golfer. So he was not only a good partner for Ola, he was a good golf partner for me.

Chris and Ola's Charleston was the iconic moment of the series. That was a wonderful dance that you could see in any stage show. The response from the audience was phenomenal. They chose it for their final and people couldn't wait to see it again, so that was my favourite. I always go with the majority!

Ola was very clever at the choreography, and Chris is so adaptable. Who would think this guy, who is a very good sports presenter on *BBC Breakfast* could win the show? But he is a good sportsman – he plays cricket, he plays football and golf very well – and sportsmen adapt well to *Strictly Come Dancing* because they have a very good sense of timing, and they have control of all their limbs and hands. I hope the BBC furthers his career – he deserves it.

Having said that, the contestant that I was the most disappointed in, because she didn't get further than the first week, was Martina Hingis. I thought she looked wonderful and I thought she was going to be very good, so I couldn't believe that she went out so soon. Sometimes these things happen and it's difficult to find a reason but it was a shame.

I was very sorry to see Jade drop out due to injury because she's a Johnson, and people who saw me on *Who Do You Think You Are?* will know my full name is Bruce Joseph Forsyth Johnson. When we were in Blackpool, and she did that wonderful jive with Ian Waite, I said, 'By the way, I'm a Johnson as well' and she was really intrigued with that. But I was very disappointed for her because she could have been a finalist, very easily. It was a great shame, just as it was when Kelly Brook had to drop out and, again, she was a probable finalist. She could definitely have won it.

Last year saw our return to Blackpool for the first time since series 2. It's always good to go to Blackpool because of the atmosphere in the Tower Ballroom. We have an audience there of about 500 more than we get in the studio and the atmosphere you get from an audience is mainly down to the volume of people. Instead

of a small round of applause you hear a great big round of applause and, of course, it makes laughs bigger which is always comforting and gratifying. The building is beautiful and is built for ballroom dancing so it's the perfect place to dance – it is the home of ballroom.

Having Alesha on board was interesting because she could give her opinion and her marks based on the experience of being a champion. She knows what the contestants are going through and how many hours they spend training and rehearsing, so she could voice a different opinion from the other judges. She was very nervous on the first show, but anyone would be. She got stronger and stronger as the year went on and I think she found her feet very well. They were at the end of her long legs. Doing a number with Alesha, as I did in the semi-finals, was wonderful. She is professional to work with and our song-and-dance number went very well. It was a highlight for me.

The last series also saw three additional dances, in the Charleston, Lindy hop and rock 'n' roll, and I think they helped the show. Anything new you can put in, like the Argentine tango and the salsa in series 4, keeps it fresh. Variety of the dances can always give the show a slightly different look. Of course, my biggest disappointment of last year was missing a live show for the first time since the series began, because I was suffering with flu. It felt very strange indeed watching the show at home; I was just glad that Ronnie Corbett wasn't taller than me! And being the little trouper that he is, he saved the day, as well as Tess and Claudia who did a marvellous job.

I'm looking forward to the show returning with fourteen new celebrities this year. With two less couples, the show will breathe a bit easier, especially in the early weeks. I hope you are as excited as I am about the new line-up. See you on Saturday night – and don't forget to…
Keeeep Dancing!

Daly THOUGHTS

The last series of *Strictly Come Dancing* was a corker and I absolutely loved it. What drama! There was never a dull moment, what with the injuries to Jade, Laila and Ali, Bruce being ill and missing the show and going back to Blackpool, the home of ballroom, which we all love.

What I enjoyed most about last year, though, is that it wasn't a foregone conclusion, even towards the end. No one could predict the winner. Would it be Ricky? Would it be Chris? It was a nailbiter right down to the show dance, and it literally came down to that.

We had all standards last year. We had Ricky Whittle, who was absolutely excellent from the off, without a doubt a naturally talented dancer. Then we had Chris Hollins who no one could have ever predicted making it to the final, let alone taking the trophy. In weeks one to four, you wouldn't have said he was a finalist, but of course he went on 'the journey', came out a champ, and surprised himself and everybody else while he was at it. Who could have predicted the 'dancing Hobbit' would go all the way to the title?

As a couple they had great chemistry together and they genuinely adored each other, which was very evident. As the friendship grew so did his dancing skills and his confidence, and he really got into it. He wanted to get better and he wanted to get to the next stage of the competition. Chris was moving house and working, getting up at four in the morning, but he wouldn't sacrifice the training. He

set his eye on the goal and he made it. He was the people's champ because he was the ordinary guy who couldn't dance and suddenly, he picked up his dancing skills and pulled it out the bag!

Chris and Ola's Charleston was one of those brilliant moments when your jaw just drops to the floor and the choreography was absolute genius. But I also loved watching Jo Wood because I just adored her. She was so sweet and she tried so hard. She's not the greatest dancer in the world, given, but she was a real trier and she so wanted to please Brendan. And she brought out a whole new nurturing side to Brendan that we'd never seen before. She softened him up because he saw how hard she was trying to please him but she just couldn't grasp it.

The saddest moment for me was Jade Johnson having to bow out. She was a real tomboy and then *Strictly* got into her blood and she became a lady, which even amazed her. She said she'd grown out of being a tomboy and she felt she'd gone through a personal transformation. She had fallen in love with dance, and discovered a whole new side to herself, but then she had to crash out. She was absolutely devastated and you couldn't help but feel for her because she genuinely didn't want to leave and she was an incredible dancer.

A bout of flu meant Bruce missed his first show ever but in these cases the show must go on no matter what. The producer told me, 'All right, it's your turn. You're up front. Claudia is coming to help and she's backstage.' We were like two giggly girls at school having fun while the teacher's away! We missed Bruce though. It was nerve-racking at the beginning without him. Ronnie Corbett, Bruce's mate and a big fan of the show, came along to help us out, but it almost ended in disaster before it had begun when he tripped at the top of the stairs at the start of the show. I thought it was a joke, so I was standing there laughing and then I realised that it wasn't a comedy fall, it was an actual fall. Luckily, he regained his composure like the true pro he is and the show went on. We also had a bit of fun taking the mickey out of the usual opening of the show, where I kick my leg out and Bruce catches it, but we did it with Ronnie and I caught *his* leg. His wee leg was so tiny, I had to bend down in my high heels to reach it and it was hilarious.

The last series marked my return to work after the birth of my second baby, Amber. I was quite clever with the timing, although it wasn't intentional. It was a happy coincidence that Amber came along at the end of May, which fits in with the series perfectly – how considerate of her!

After being knee deep in nappies, it was a complete and utter treat to be spoilt again. I got the chance to dress up and be girly, be pampered a little bit before the show, and grab an hour of 'me time' before it all got crazy again and we went live.

Even after seven series, I still can't wait for that new list of celebrities to come through. While you can't predict who will be the dancers and who will have two left feet, seeing the final names after all the rumours and the speculation is still one of the most exciting moments of the whole process.

I'm looking forward to watching them all as they get the *Strictly* bug. Last year, as I said, there was drama in bucketloads. I don't know if I'm hoping for a calmer ride this year or not!

THE STORY OF SERIES 7

✦ Week 1

Tango Tussle

It was all change in the *Strictly* camp as series 7 opened with each couple performing two dances in their first week, on two live shows. Len declared how delighted he was to be sitting next to new judge Alesha rather than Bruno 'because I had a perforated left ear last time'. Bulky presenter Rav Wilding managed to split his trousers before splitting the judges over his tango, causing the first row of the series between Len and Craig and receiving a paltry 3 from the Aussie judge.

Face Off

Alesha and Bruno were soon battling it out over Chris Hollins's facial expressions. Although the panel were impressed with his tango, Bruno accused the *BBC Breakfast* presenter of looking like he was 'sucking a lemon', which prompted singer Alesha to jump to his defence. Ali and Brian pulled off an elegant waltz, which Alesha called 'classic, beautiful' and Craig declared, 'fab-u-lous', and bagged a whopping 30 for their first dance.

Saucy Madam

Oxo mum Lynda Bellingham was so shocked when Craig said her tango had been 'the longest one minute thirty ever' that she asked, 'Would you like more sauce in your gravy?' Despite losing her footing tennis player Martina Hingis served up a passable waltz; during her version of the same dance athlete Jade Johnson smiled her way through a 'first-class' attempt. Was Joe Calzaghe punching above his weight after struggling with his tango? Len certainly thought so, describing the boxer's Latin moves as something 'only a mother could love'.

Jade Jumps to It

In rehearsal, Jade admitted *Strictly* was tougher than the Olympics, saying, 'With long jump I get six attempts. With *Strictly* I only get one.' But she managed a sizzling cha-cha-cha that impressed the judges and ended in the splits. 'Nasty and naughty and I loved it,' gushed Bruno.

Ali's Arresting Rumba

The Bill star Ali Bastian and partner Brian Fortuna delivered a sultry rumba that thrilled everyone but Len, who complained about the 'posing and posturing'. Alesha called Ali 'one of the most beautiful dancers I've ever seen', and Craig said he loved it, prompting Len's tart response, 'You would, you're from Camden.' Len also explained that the rumba was the 'story of a developing romance'. It certainly was for Ali and Brian!

Week 2

Nerves and Niggles

The remaining eight celebrities took centre stage for their ballroom and nerves were sky high. Natalie Cassidy said she was 'terrified', but pleased the judges with her attack in the tango, despite partner Vincent Simone standing on her dress. Bruce asked Craig if he was in a better mood this week, following his score of 2 for Joe, and Craig replied, 'I'm always in a good mood – until the dances start.' Oh dear.

Game, Set and Match

EastEnder Ricky Groves won the audience's heart with a cha-cha-cha that had Bruno asking, 'Did you have rocket fuel for lunch?' Joe's Latin was less than knockout, earning him a 2 from Craig and leaving him bottom of the table with 32 points, while Ali topped it with 60. Martina took time off from training to pass on a few tennis tips to partner Matthew Cutler, but her rumba saw her facing Rav in the dance off. With a tie-break decision going to Len, the tennis player crashed out of the tournament.

WAGs at Forty Paces

Former *Footballers' Wives* rivals Laila Rouass and Zoe Lucker were pitted against each other for their first dance. 'I have got to kick Zoe's butt,' Laila said in training. 'Zoe, you're going down, girlfriend.' Zoe's waltz won the judges over and Bruno commented, 'The evil queen of WAGs is transformed into the picture of elegance and poise.' Laila's tingling tango had Alesha declaring it 'wicked!', tying Laila and Zoe on 30 each.

Ricky Steals the Show

The WAGs' triumph was short-lived. *Hollyoaks* star Ricky Whittle swept to the top of the table with an astonishing waltz that earned him 33 points. 'You're the one to beat,' Len told Ricky, and Bruno said, 'A dream come true. The most stunning debut from anyone we've ever had.' Jo Wood struggled with the tango, after falling backwards over a box in training, but in the group dance performed to a Michael Jackson hit, Ricky Groves revealed a hidden talent with a perfect moonwalk.

Judges Not Bowled Over

The second night for the second group saw them tackling the Latin, and cricketer Phil Tufnell, who had even impressed Craig with his waltz, went 'from magic to tragic', as Len put it, with his cha-cha-cha. As in the first week group dance, his tongue came in for criticism with Craig commenting that it 'saw more action than your hips'. 'I need facial choreography,' joked the bowler.

Footballer's Wife Scores

Laila disappointed Bruno with a tepid cha-cha-cha, prompting his comment, 'Yesterday I was crazy for you. Now I want a divorce.' While Zoe struggled with the idea of being sexy in rumba rehearsals, come Saturday night, Len accused her of being 'over-raunchy'. Bruno, however, 'felt something growing, big and powerful', and Craig added, 'It was like looking through a keyhole at a private moment.' Phew!

Richard Rides into the Sunset

Ricky Whittle proved he was no one-trick pony with a raunchy rumba that had Alesha 'blown away'. He finished top of the table with 65 points. Darcey Bussell gave the group a ballet lesson to help them loosen up, much to Phil's amusement, but unfortunately it wasn't enough to help Jo and Brendan avoid the bottom of the scoreboard. They escaped the dance off, and jockey Richard Dunwoody was pipped at the post when all three judges voted to keep in Craig Kelly. 'You have definitely been the most hard-working partner I've had,' said Lilia, adding that, 'The best thing out of it is that I am finally going to learn how to ride horses!'

Week 3

Slip Sliding Away

With the first weeks out of the way the celebs had just one routine to learn – and the slip-up ratio was sky high. Chris fluffed the quickstep and quipped, 'You would have loved the original routine!' before receiving a disappointing 23. Anton was thrilled by last week's score and joked, 'Fifty-five in the first week! I reckon if you totted up the total of all my previous series, I wouldn't get fifty-five.' Sadly this week, Laila's footwork 'went to pieces'. Despite this, they still scored 30 for their quickstep. Craig, however, scored just 21 after his ballroom disaster.

Wear and Tear

Although it was only the third week, the celebs had been in training for seven weeks and the strain was beginning to show. Natalie Cassidy was caught napping in rehearsal. 'The choreography is quite hard and she has been exhausted,' said worried partner Vincent, while Phil Tufnell was bowled over with a knee injury.

From Ravishing to Rav

Ricky Whittle struck again with a moody paso which had Alesha gasping, 'I have never seen anyone in the history of *Strictly Come Dancing* come out and do a paso like that! I loved it.' Ali's quickstep was a triumph and her romance with Brian was out in the open. 'There was a lack of body contact and from what I've read in the papers, that really did surprise me,' laughed Len. Lynda remarked that in her paso doble: 'It may well be a bull, but as far as I'm concerned it's a stroppy cow.' At the end of the evening *Crimewatch*'s Rav was out after a quickstep that managed to incorporate a cartwheel.

12

Week 4

The Cat Licks His Wounds

Cricketer Phil started off the week in hospital, having keyhole surgery for a torn cartilage in his knee. He managed to make it back to training by Tuesday and by Saturday he was shaking his tailfeather in a salsa that Alesha said made 'great usage of the buttocks area'. Bruno used a more fruity anatomical word and Phil hobbled off with a respectable 24. Jade's salsa proved even saucier when a handstand resulted in a little fallout. 'It was an eye opener!' joked Len.

Sleeping Beauties

Laila took a leaf out of Natalie's book, bedding down among the gym equipment in a cupboard. She woke up in time for a foxy foxtrot, which Craig labelled 'classy and confident'. Laila and Anton bagged their first 9 and the coveted top spot with a high score of 34.

Joe Fights On

Joe's dad Enzo paid a visit to him in training and said, 'I'm proud of him. Not because he's a great fighter but because he's a wonderful kid.' But the boxer still finished joint last with Jo Wood, on 20.

Following a tough week of filming *Hollyoaks*, Ricky's crown slipped and he ended in joint third with Ali. After being reduced to tears last week, Craig ended up in the dance off with Lynda. But it was on the actress that the curtain closed.

Week 5

Jive Talking

Ricky Groves went from Albert Square to Times Square as he kicked off his jive with a hepcat comb and a dodgy American accent, watched by his 92-year-old gran. Ali and Brian's jive told the story of a rocky relationship as the American boy sat on the lap of a surprised audience member. But it ended in tears after Ali slipped and received her first score under 30. And it was 'Oh dear, baby' when Chris and Ola hit a low, receiving just 22 points for their attempt.

Bruno Wings It

Jade's Viennese waltz had Bruno carried away, yelling, 'It was like watching two great frigatebirds, gliding over the summer ocean, taken by the swell, taken right into the sunset. Take me with you – I'm yours!' Jade matched Ricky's week one high score of 35, only to have him soar slightly higher when he received 36 for the same dance – and landed the first 10 of the series from Alesha.

Ian is Jaded

After a tough week of training with samba king Ian, Jade lost her temper over a 'stupid little move' and refused to carry on. After the gift of a flower, the pair kissed and made up for a Saturday salsa that reversed the roles and saw Jade flinging her partner around the floor, prompting Bruno to shout, 'You fierce exotic Amazon!' But a score of 32 couldn't keep her out of the dance off.

Bad Boy Brendan is Back

Brendan was hopping mad when Bruno compared Jo Wood to a grasshopper and Craig upped the ante by calling her 'a bush kangaroo'. Storming off in a fury, Brendan ranted, 'It's Craig's ignorance and lack of knowledge of the dance that lets him say things like that to this lovely girl.' Joe's jive was considered 'a vast improvement' by Craig but, after a dance off against Zoe, the boxer was knocked out.

✦ Week 6 ✦

Say it with T-shirts

Chris's jive disaster meant Ola was back to being Mrs Jordan and the only 'Yeah baby' he was getting was on his newly printed Team Cola T-shirt. Tuffers expressed his feelings with 'I'm NOT a Samba Man' emblazoned across his chest. And Craig felt much the same way after brother Dean Lennox Kelly popped into rehearsal and proved quite good at the dance. 'It's embarrassing,' said the *Corrie* star, before a 'nightmare' samba left him with just 18 points.

Ali and the Smooth American

Ali's American smooth with her smooth American hit the spot and a delighted Bruno told her, 'I've been waiting six weeks for this. It's magic time!' At the other end of the scale, Jo, the ex-wife of a Rolling Stone, hit rock bottom and was accused of 'dragging Brendan into samba hell'. With 14, the lowest samba score ever, and Jade as the opponent in the dance off, how could she 'Not Fade Away'?

Lucker's Luck Runs Out

Ricky Whittle's quickstep earned him three 10s and the highest score of the series so far, with 39. Ali was in agony after badly bruising her toe in rehearsal, but she made it through the paso before being carried offstage by Brian. She scored an impressive 33, but ended up in a shock dance off against Zoe, whose samba had Bruno bubbling with excitement and earned her 32. The judges were furious and Len called the dance off 'ludicrous'.

Week 7

Little and Large

Natalie Cassidy finally got to perform her favourite dance, the jive, and at the opening of the show Bruce joked, 'I told Natalie that the fast-and-furious jive could really wear you down. She asked, "What do you mean?" and I said, "When Vincent first started doing it he was six foot four." Then he looked at the tiny couple and added, 'Who put him next to Jade and Ian? Look at them!' But the actress felt like a giant after receiving a coveted 30 points.

Licence to Thrill

Ricky G revealed an obsession with James Bond and confessed, 'It's a bit over the top. I have about two and a half thousand bits and pieces.' But after his Bond-themed rumba, Craig called the dance 'conceited', and Len looked like he wanted a licence to kill. As he berated his fellow judge, Craig told Len to stop pointing. 'I'll do more than point in a minute,' Len retorted. Ricky scored 24 – including a 007 from Alesha.

Week 8

Ballroom Blitz

The show decamped to Blackpool's Tower Ballroom and the trip saw a rise in the fortunes for two couples in particular. After Craig's comments that his hands were 'splayed', Chris spent all week with his fingers taped together and scored a whopping 34 for his foxtrot. With an ever-cheerful Craig bemused that he could find nothing at all to criticise, Ali nabbed the ultimate score of 40, the highest ever for a Viennese waltz. Bruno summed it up as, 'A magic venue, an enchanting dance.'

Jade Gives Len a Thrill

Ian came face to face with six life-sized models of Jade when she took him back to her old school. Her headmistress revealed that 'Jade was not a perfect student', but admitted she had become a 'fantastic role model'. An energetic jive left Len tingling, thanks to the bouncy floor. 'As you bounced it went through my chair and right into my bottom,' he laughed. 'My false teeth fell out and it was the most exciting moment!'

Craig Comes Home

Blackpool is not only the home of ballroom, but the hometown of Craig Kelly, who had set his sights on dancing in the famous ballroom. His family turned out to support him, and he promised, 'I'm going to go out there like this is my last dance.' But his cha-cha-cha fell flat and Alesha drew gasps when she blasted, 'I'm happy you got to Blackpool, Craig, but I can't believe Zoe's gone and I had to endure that!' Ouch! A crestfallen Craig scored 17 and left the competition.

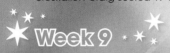

Ronnie Gets Brucie Bonus

For the first time since *Strictly* began, Bruce Forsyth was forced to miss a show after he was struck down with flu. Old pal Ronnie Corbett stepped into the breach to help Tess out front, while an excited Claudia Winkleman took over Tess's backstage area. And that wasn't the only drama on the show.

Sad Jade Sits Out

After sustaining a serious knee injury in rehearsal, doctors told a tearful Jade that her tango was a no-no. 'I feel like I'm letting Ian down and everyone who has supported us. I just really wanted to do this dance.' She wasn't the only one suffering, either. After Laila tripped on the stairs and twisted her ankle, she vowed to carry on with her samba. But she had to stop halfway through the routine when the pain got too much.

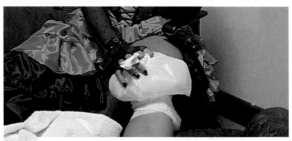

Judges Put the Cat Out

Ricky G wore specs to get into character for his Viennese waltz, but it couldn't keep Ricky W and Ali from bagging their usual spots at the top of the table. This week, Natalie Cassidy was proving to be a serious contender, just one point behind the two leaders, scoring 34 points with a sexy samba. Phil's knee had swelled up but he managed an American smooth that impressed the judges and earned his best score yet. Unfortunately, the dance off with Ricky and Erin saw Phil and Katya bowled out.

Week 10

Jade Bows Out

Laila was back after her injury but she missed out on three days of training. 'I've been given the go ahead but I've only got three days to do it.' More unluckily, Jade was forced to quit the show over fears she would ruin her chances to compete in the Olympics in 2012. 'It's very emotional for me,' the athlete admitted from her audience seat. 'Just sitting here is really hard for me.'

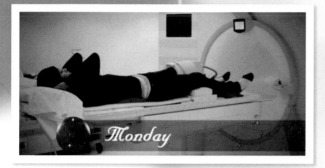

Incredible Hulk and the Incredible Sulk

Ricky Whittle told partner Natalie that 'The Incredible Hulk would struggle with these lifts' and his bench-press lift in the American smooth led to raised voices on the panel. Bruno called him 'a romantic soul with the strength of Samson', Len called the lift 'incongruous' and Craig argued that it was all in the song: 'She was singing about "over the rainbow" – up she goes, over the rainbow,' and called Len 'D-U-double-L, Dull'. Len responded with a petulant, 'I don't even want to argue with him because he's such a doughnut.'

Square Dance

EastEnder Natalie treated Vincent to a tour of Albert Square and impressed her co-stars with a twirl or two outside the Queen Vic. 'It's been great coming back with Vincent to the place I really feel is home,' she said. However, the trip didn't help her score, which at 26 was her lowest since week one. Chris took ballet lessons to help his Viennese waltz, and EastEnder Ricky Groves made his exit after a dance off with Laila.

Week 11

Chris Fools Around

'We're down to the last five, which is incredible,' marvelled Chris. It was a tough week, with the couples learning new dances in either the Charleston and rock 'and' roll as well as a group Viennese waltz, which was to be judged for the first time. And Chris was moving house. He still managed to pull the right moves on the dance floor and prove the Charleston really was his dance as Bruno called him, 'The delightful dancing fool at his best.'

Darcey Bussells In

With the arrival of ballerina Darcey Bussell, *Strictly* had five judges for the first time ever, and four couples were vying to be the first to score 50. Ricky came closest with a foxtrot to 'Too Marvellous', which proved to be just that, scoring 48 and an 'a-maz-ing' from Craig. His cheeky cha-cha-cha charmed the female judges into giving him a 10, and Alesha told him, 'It was flirty, it was sexy – we were getting a bit excited here.' And after Craig's cracks about his pigeon toes, Ricky was thrilled to hear 'Sexy, masculine – and turned out!'

Fabulous Flapper

Chris was thrilled with his score of 34, but he was soon trumped by Ali. Despite a painful twisted ankle, her *Chicago*-inspired number scored 37 – including a 10 from Alesha who called it 'kooky and quirky' and added, 'After the week you've had that was outstanding.' And *The Bill* star managed to pick up another 10 in the group Viennese, leaving her top of the table again.

Happy Days and Tearful Nights

During training for the rock 'n' roll Ricky received a visit from The Fonz, AKA *Strictly* fan Henry Winkler. But it wasn't *happy days* for the *Hollyoaks* hunk, starting with an energetic routine to master and ending with mistakes in the live performance that left him with his first 7 and his lowest score to date. Natalie's dance turned into rock and no roll, as Vincent was too scared to do a roly poly and the judges complained the routine was 'one-dimensional'. After losing in a dance off with Laila, the popular actress was in tears as she received a lengthy ovation from the audience.

Face the Music

Chris's facial expressions caused another barney on the judges' panel after Craig told him 'the strain started to show on your face'. Angry Alesha said, 'We need to get over the face thing now.' Len claimed 'it was romance', but Bruno jumped out of his seat to insist it was 'lemon-sucking time'. The samba unleashed a beast in the mild-mannered sports presenter who shimmied, shook and waved his booty in the face of a shocked audience member. He did kiss her hand and apologise afterwards though!

18

Dizzy Heights

The judges went all hip-hop when they urged Ali to 'bring sexy back', but after the tango, Len called her a 'one-trick pony' and 'only able to do elegant'. She proved him wrong with a samba that Darcey dubbed 'a sexy party'. Having made the final stages, Anton joked, 'I feel like I've sneaked in to somebody else's party. I feel a bit giddy.' Laila felt even giddier after the lifts in the American smooth and she messed up her salsa, scoring just 59 points for the two. A shock audience poll left top ranker Ricky in the dance off against Laila, and the actress was out.

Waltzing Whittle

Ricky was shaken by his close shave in the quarter-finals, and admitted, 'To go from the top of the table to the dance off is frightening.' But his waltz prompted a rare standing ovation from the professionals, and had Darcey raving, 'Ricky, you are pure class.' He topped that with an Argentine tango which Alesha declared, 'Sexy, hot, passionate, intense. That made the hairs on my arms stand up.' Craig was even booed for giving him a 9, but Ricky still topped the board with 49 and 96 for the two dances.

Ali and Out

Training for the Argentine tango and the American smooth was tough for Ali and she tearfully told Brian, 'I'm completely broken. It's not even stress any more.' Her tango suffered but she still scored 42. Emotions ran high in her second dance, the American smooth, as Ali made *Strictly* history with the first ever 50. Sadly, it didn't stop her falling victim to the public vote but at least she could waltz off into the sunset with her American boy, who told her, 'You've made this season absolutely magical for me.' Sweet!

Week 13: The Semi-Finals

Fishing for Compliments

As Jade left early, three couples were through to the semis, and the dance off was scrapped. The judges and public scores combined would decide who would go. Chris joked, 'I'm in the semi-finals! What the hell happened?', and Ola wept with joy at getting through. Their rumba failed to impress Craig and Darcey but their mood improved with the Argentine tango. 'The trout mouth is certainly back but I'm starting to find it endearing, oddly,' said Craig.

19

The Grand Final

Match of the Day

Chris and Ricky went head-to-head for the famous glitterball trophy but before the contest began they faced each other on the hallowed turf of Wembley Stadium. Chris jibed, 'It's David versus Goliath. It's the hunk versus the hobbit. And we might just do a bit of giant slaying tonight.' But with four dances, including a joint Lindy hop and a show dance to learn, there was all to play for. And while the judges were awarding points, who won the seventh series of *Strictly* would come down purely to the public vote.

Charleston Champ

Their foxtrot earned them 46, but Chris and Ola received their first perfect score with the Charleston, which Bruno called 'a *Strictly Come Dancing* classic'. 'This is turning into the best final ever!' said Len. 'It's a classic confrontation: the dancer and the entertainer.' After a shared Lindy hop, which Chris nailed by a point, and a show dance, Team Cola were four points behind Ricky on 186. The public chose the entertainer and Chris lifted the trophy, but not before thanking Ricky and Natalie for being good sports. His warmest words were for a tearful 'Olachops'. 'Thank you so much for believing in me all along,' he said. 'I did test you a little bit but thank you so much.'

Ricky is on Thong

The *Hollyoaks* hunk promised to wear a thong if he reached the final and wardrobe had provided a crystal-studded one emblazoned with his name. But the quickstep called for more elegant attire, and Ricky even impressed Craig, getting his first perfect score after 16 weeks. 'Danced like a champion,' said Bruno. The repeat cha-cha-cha had Darcey feeling 'hot', and Bruno declaring, 'This is a dance competition – and *boy*, you can dance!'

20

NEW DANCES
the charleston

It was a mainstay of speakeasies in the 1920s, but series 7 was the first time the Charleston made it on to the *Strictly Come Dancing* floor. And current champ Chris Hollins has already set a gold standard for future competitors, bagging a perfect score of 50 in the final.

Although it has similarities to a dance known as the branle, which dates back as far as the sixteenth century, the Charleston was thought to have been devised in the early twentieth century by African-Americans in the southern part of the United States. But its popularity spread like wildfire among the rebellious white women who frequented the illicit drinking clubs that sprung up during the Prohibition of the 1920s. As it was considered an immoral dance by many, the flappers of the era would delight in dancing alone or in groups as another way to thumb their noses at the 'drys'.

Charleston competitions were widespread in America and many famous actresses, including Joan Crawford and Ginger Rogers, used them as stepping stones to a career in movies.

In the late twenties, a new dance called the black bottom swept the nation and briefly replaced the Charleston. However, the Charleston's popularity was to revive in later years and many of the steps were incorporated into more modern dances such as the Lindy hop and the mashed potato.

The steps appeared in several Broadway shows including the *Ziegfield Follies of 1922* and the 1923 Irvin C. Miller production *Liza*. But its name and mainstream popularity was derived from the James P. Johnson song 'Charleston', written for the 1923 show *Runnin' Wild*, which became one of the biggest hits of the decade. Composer Johnson claimed he had first heard the characteristic beat from dockers in Charleston, South Carolina.

Len on the Charleston

'When I first heard that the Charleston was going to be part of *Strictly Come Dancing* I was horrified,' says traditionalist Len Goodman. 'Again, as many times before on this show, I was proved wrong because I felt it brought a really fun element into *Strictly*.

'I'm an old fuddy-duddy ballroom and Latin person so if it goes outside of the ten traditional dances – five ballroom and five Latin – then I'm always going to raise an eyebrow. But I must say that I felt it brought a different dynamic and a fresh challenge, not only to the celebrities but also to the

professionals, because they're not dances that they would normally have trained for or even done before.

'It brought a new edge to the whole thing, with us wondering whether the pros would be able to pull it off. And they were fun dances, which isn't a bad thing.'

the lindy hop

The Lindy hop is named in honour of Charles Lindbergh's Atlantic Crossing in 1927 and derived many of its steps from the Charleston of a few years earlier, as well as the Texas Tommy and the breakaway.

The dance first emerged in Harlem, New York, when jazz was in its heyday. One particularly popular Harlem venue, the Savoy Ballroom, soon became notorious, with young whites turning up to watch the black dancers' latest steps. The best hoofers would meet in 'Kat's Corner' and take it in turns to show off their skills and the manager soon began to pay them to dance. According to jazz poet Langston Hughes, this led to the Lindy hop becoming increasingly acrobatic. 'The Lindy hoppers at the Savoy even began to practise acrobatic routines, and to do absurd things for the entertainment of the whites, that probably never would have entered their heads to attempt for their own effortless amusement,' he said.

However, it wasn't until the mid-1930s that the 'air steps' – such as the hip to hip, the side flip and the over the back, in which the lady's feet both leave the ground – were introduced by a new generation of Lindy hoppers, led by dance instructor Frankie Manning. Savoy bouncer Herbert White also put together his own troupe, known as Whitey's Lindy Hoppers, who took the dance around the country and even featured in Hollywood movies, such as *Hellzapoppin'* and *A Day at the Races*. By the end of the thirties the mainstream dance schools, including the world-famous Arthur Murray School, began to teach it in their studios.

The forties brought the Lindy to UK shores, along with the US soldiers stationed on British soil, but in its homeland a heavy tax on dance halls in the war years saw it dip in popularity. In the 1980s a revival began in Cameron Dance Center in New York, after they tracked down Frankie Manning and fellow Lindy legend Al Minns, who was instrumental in setting up the New York Swing Dance Society. Today the Lindy is danced by enthusiasts in clubs around the world.

The Grand Final in December 2009 saw the dance enter the *Strictly* record book, with Ricky and Natalie and Chris and Ola dancing it together for the first time on the show. While strong Ricky's lifts were more impressive, the style of the dance was more suited to Chris, according to Craig. 'This really is a dance for Hobbits – dancers at the smaller end of the spectrum,' he said. With a score of 44 Chris pipped Ricky at the post by one point.

rock 'n' roll

While Bill Haley was rocking around the clock, in the 1950s, the Lindy hop was morphing into the jive and the more acrobatic version, known as the rock 'n' roll.

While the jive maintained some of the sharper kicks and flicks of the Lindy, the rock 'n' roll was a more freestyle, expressive dance with plenty of throws, jumps and lifts that could be performed by couples or groups of between four and eight couples.

Typical moves include the body wave, used by the man to raise a girl from sitting position on the floor, and the swan, which sees the girl raised above the man's head with her legs pointed upwards. When the dance was introduced on *Strictly Come Dancing* for the first time in series 7, Len was looking forward to, 'girls spinning around, a flash of knickers, whoo hoo. Anything goes'. But the couples performing this fared much worse than those who had been given the Charleston, and even Ricky Whittle messed up one of the moves and was told by Len that 'it could have done with a little more freedom'. Natalie and Vincent had trouble with the acrobatics and their routine was dismissed by Craig as 'very one-dimensional'.

Len on the Rock 'n' Roll and Lindy Hop

'The Charleston, because it's not a proper dance, is judged more on the fun element and I was hoping we would be able to do the same on the rock 'n' roll and the Lindy hop. However, the pros are steeped in jive and it was very difficult for them to get away from what they've trained for. So they all had a slightly jivey look to them, rather than being a free-spirited dance.

'The jive has more flicks and kicks but they were allowed to do lifts and throws in these dances, so I would have liked to have seen more of that going on in the rock 'n' roll and Lindy hop. They came along

quite late in the series and the pros and celebrities are getting tired, so I don't think the rock 'n' roll had as much energy as the Charleston, which seemed to be more free spirited.

'It's very difficult to judge these dances other than for entertainment, especially for me because I judge on the fundamental principles of the dances that I know. When it goes out of those parameters, I have to judge it on the entertainment value, the fun and the enjoyment it gives me, so I almost become one of the viewers.'

As a former *Blue Peter* presenter Matt Baker is always up for a challenge. He recently travelled from Kazakhstan to Mongolia as part of Children in Need's *Around The World In 80 Days* and while on *Blue Peter* he broke the hang-gliding record for the highest altitude towed launch. As a huge fan of the show, he is delighted to be given the chance to dance.

'*Strictly* is something I have watched every season and have always said that it would be something I

presented *City Hospital, Animal Rescue Squad* and *Country File* as well as commentating on gymnastics on *Grandstand*. He is also a regular commentator on gymnastics for BBC2 and the London Marathon for BBC1.

Now dad to Luke and Molly, and living in Hertfordshire, the former gymnast reckons he might be a bit out of shape.

'It's funny, as I went to a stag do the other night and was thinking that I have not danced in ages,' he says. 'I have got two kids aged three and one and so have

MATT BAKER

would love to do and now the opportunity has arisen I jumped at it,' he comments. '*Strictly* is such a big institution and my whole family are huge fans and for them to be part of it as well is wonderful.'

As well as a foxy foxtrot, viewers can expect a few tricks and acrobatics from the former British gymnastics champ.

'I was a gymnast for many years and to help I did little bits and pieces of dance training. Ballet training in gymnastics always helps. I have also been in the musical *Chitty Chitty Bang Bang* on tour so did a bit of dancing in that.'

Matt was born in Durham and grew up on the family sheep farm with his sister and two stepsisters. After a sporty career at school Matt missed out on a career in physiotherapy as he didn't get the grades, so he chose drama and signed up to Queen Margaret University, Edinburgh, to do an acting degree. After two years he was offered a job on *Blue Peter* and gave up the course.

As part of the *Blue Peter* team for seven years, he trained as a stuntman, slept in jungles and lived as a nomad in Morocco, and these exciting adventures also landed him two BAFTA awards for Best Children's Presenter. Since leaving the show in 2006, he has

not been nightclubbing for ages, and am worried that I will have turned into "dad dancing" now. I am also really unfit at the moment so am looking forward to getting back in shape. I have spent half my life doing gymnastics so am hoping there will be muscle memory.'

But it's his mental memory that he's more worried about. 'I am quite coordinated and I would say I have got a bit of rhythm. The trouble I have is remembering and I am worried I will forget the routines, and because you have a partner it's going to be very difficult to freestyle if I do.'

The 32-year-old presenter is a free-spirited type and feels the ballroom might be a little too formal for his liking. 'I reckon I will be more of a Latin boy because I think it's a bit freer,' he reveals. 'Ballroom is quite fixed and restrictive. I like to be cheesy and freak out, and in fact my main problem is that I may be too cheesy. I love the jive, though, as it's happy and I am looking forward to having a go at that.

'The rumba is one that seems quite traumatic. I get a bit dizzy when I spin a lot so the Viennese waltz might be a problem too.'

Used to being a high achiever, Matt is surprisingly laid back about his hopes for the competition and is happy just to be taking part.

'I would like to have a go at the jive,' he admits. 'I just hope I don't let myself down as I want to get quite far in the competition. I hope, at least, I stay out of the bottom two for a few weeks. I would be lying if I said I did not want to win but when you watch the programme it looks brilliant to be part of it. I know lots of people who have already taken part and they all say what an amazing experience it is and I am so looking forward to throwing myself into it.

'I hope I stay in long enough for all my family and friends to be able to come down and watch the show,' he says. 'Obviously I want to have a great time on the show but I also know that there is a job to do…and that's to get as far as I can.'

lead judge *len*

Ballroom king Len Goodman was impressed by many of the celebrity dancers in the seventh season of *Strictly Come Dancing*, although, in typically eloquent style, he compares the whole series to a Clint Eastwood movie.

'What I liked about this series is that it was truly the good, the bad and the ugly,' he laughs. 'There were some really good ones, some very bad ones and a few ugly scenes along the way.

'Overall there were some absolutely wonderful stand-out performances. There were some wonderful jewels among it all and there were some pretty awful dancers too.'

As head judge, Len had a new member on his team, in the stunning shape of Alesha Dixon. The singer and winner of *Strictly* series 5 added new spice to the judges' comments and Len felt she dealt with her position as new girl extremely well.

'Alesha was marvellous,' he says. 'She was under a lot of pressure and she did a very good job. She's in a unique position in that she has actually competed on *Strictly Come Dancing*, and I felt her critiques were just right. She could relate to the pressures and the problems the dancers were experiencing and that helped them.'

Len is looking forward to a new series this year and believes fewer dancers will make for better viewing.

'I think it's a very good thing we only have fourteen this year,' he says. 'I still get quite excited when the list of celebrities is sent to me and I'm really glad we have no inkling until everyone else knows. It's a bit like a new menu. It's nice to see some dishes that reassure you, like steak and chips, but it's also not a bad thing if there are a few things you are not quite sure of but sound as though they could be delicious!'

AFTER LYNDA BELLINGHAM'S TANGO

'There was drama and passion but you need more movement – it was as though both legs were down one hole of your knickers.'

AFTER RICKY WHITTLE'S AMERICAN SMOOTH

'The whole number was absolutely gorgeously fantastic, like Leonardo da Vinci painting the Mona Lisa, then getting to the end and drawing a moustache on it. Why did you do that great big lift?'

ON CHRIS HOLLINS GETTING THROUGH TO THE QUARTER-FINALS

'He's like Bilbo Baggins. You could cuddle him.'

AFTER JADE JOHNSON'S CHA-CHA-CHA

'On occasion your posture is more bent than a politician's expenses.'

ON ALI BASTIAN'S FOXTROT

'If that was a pudding it would be an Angel Delight.'

ON MARTINA HINGIS'S WALTZ

'A bit like a doughnut with no jam. It looked tasty but it disappointed.'

ON CHRIS'S FINAL CHARLESTON

'I'll tell you what, sunshine, that was fantastic entertainment.'

len's lowdown on series 7

Who was the best dancer?

Ricky Whittle was a very good dancer. Looking back over the entire history of the show, the two best dancers who have not won *Strictly Come Dancing* were Ricky Whittle and Colin Jackson. They are the two who, after the semi-final, I would have put money on to win but never did. I do understand why Chris won, because he was very very popular and everybody was impressed with his journey. But the truth of the matter is Ricky Whittle was an exceptional dancer. That's part of the fun of *Strictly*; we put in our two pen'orth and the viewers can put in their two penn'orth, and they preferred Chris. Although the best dancer didn't win, without a doubt the one who tried the hardest, who was the most popular and the real 'charming chap' was Chris Hollins.

What was the turning point for Chris?

The Charleston was fantastic. There are always certain dances that suit couples and there are always dances, however good they are, that don't suit them. Occasionally you get one dance where it all comes together perfectly, and the music – 'Fat Sam's Grand Slam' – the choreography and the personality in the dance just makes you feel great. That was his absolute turning point and that was the moment he became a contender. Chris and Ola, who I called 'dancing Hobbits', were so cute and lovely. Chris certainly deserved to win on his pluck, his will to win and the fact that he was a very charming man.

Who else impressed you?

The standard at the top of the table was very high. There were some really outstanding ones. Ali Bastian was a beautiful dancer. Laila had her moments. Her ballroom was excellent, but she didn't really want to come out and be raunchy, so as far as her Latin American was concerned, she lacked a bit of freedom and pizzazz.

Who was the biggest surprise?

My biggest surprise was Chris Hollins. If somebody had said to me in week one that this was the eventual winner I just wouldn't have believed it possible.

Who failed to live up to expectations?

I thought Joe Calzaghe would be light on his feet, but I have already bumped into a few boxers through the show. You'd think they'd be fleet of foot, they'd bob and weave – all the things you need to be a good dancer. Poor Joe didn't have it.

Worst dancer?

Jo Wood, although you warmed to her because she had a lovely personality and we saw a new side to Brendan Cole. I never thought of him as loving, caring and sharing but he got all protective, so it was nice to see that. It's a tough choice between a few. The second week we had a dance off between Richard Dunwoody and Craig Kelly. The other three felt that Craig Kelly deserved to come back but I felt that Richard Dunwoody deserved another week. Rav was pretty bad.

He was a great muscular guy and he danced the way you would imagine a great big geezer would dance.

Favourite moment?

My overall lasting memory is of Phil Tufnell shaking his bottom on the stage in the salsa. I'm not saying that it's memorable in a good way – Tuffers' gyrating bottom still haunts my dreams!

She may have a fearsome reputation and the nickname Miss Whiplash, but elegant Erin loves a good laugh and reckons training with Ricky Groves last year gave her a barrel of them.

'Being paired with Ricky was so much fun, right from the very first moment we met,' she recalls. 'I'm so pleased we achieved ten weeks together – he really deserved it. I can't speak highly enough of Ricky and I will always remember all the laughter we had together.'

For the forthright Kiwi, ballroom was in the blood, being the daughter of two professional dancers.

'I guess like many little girls, I wanted to dance! Mum took me as a three-year-old to dance classes where I began learning ballet, tap, jazz, ballroom and Latin. Through my teens, I was also a really keen sports girl and loved many different sports – I represented my school in swimming, hockey, netball, football, trampoline and athletics.'

At fifteen, Erin travelled to Australia to watch a big competition and suddenly saw her future. 'I was

but we had just twelve hundred pounds between us. After paying a deposit on a flat and rent up front we had just one pound left!'

In 1997 she got her biggest break, when she met Anton Du Beke and became his dance partner. Within a year, the couple had danced at the Royal Albert Hall and were placed in the top 50.

'As we walked on to the floor I cried, thinking that all the hard work, sweat and tears were worth it. It's my first and best memory of Anton and me.'

After moving up through the amateur ranks, they turned professional in 2002 and immediately bagged third place at the British National Dance Championships at the Winter Gardens, Blackpool.

Having joined *Strictly* in the first series, Erin is the only female professional to have danced in all seven series and is looking forward to number eight.

'The show has opened new doors for me and given me opportunities I wouldn't have had otherwise,' she says. 'It's great to be respected as a dancer outside of the dance industry.'

bowled over, deciding right there and then that I wanted to be a serious dancer. I asked one of the professionals how I could do that.'

Three years later, she was the New Zealand Ten-Dance Amateur Champion and decided to take her dream to the rest of the world.

'At this point, my dance partner and I decided to make the big move to Sydney, Australia,' she explains. 'We lived there for eighteen months before making another move, this time even further away, to London. I remember I told my mum I'd be back within a couple of years – but here I am with still no plans to return! Coming here was the biggest adventure. At the time we thought we had loads of money,

e may not have made it to the final but Anton did achieve one ambition this year, thanks to partner Laila Rouass. Last year he joked that his hopes were 'much the same as virtually every other year – I would love to get to dance all the dances and still be in the show in November and December!' Laila took him all the way to the quarter-finals, the furthest he has been since series 1, when he reached the semis with Lesley Garrett.

that way you get more done and you want to come back tomorrow. If I tell you off and say you're rubbish you won't want to come back and that's counter-productive. Positive reinforcement is the key.'

Sevenoaks-born Anton came to dancing relatively late, at the age of fourteen, and then it was only to pick up girls! After turning up to meet his sister from her dance class he got dragged in by the tutor and there he found it was a great place to mingle with the opposite sex. He trained in Latin and ballroom for the next three years, and was quickly entered into the competition circuit.

At seventeen, he decided to specialise in ballroom. Anton maintains that Latin American dancing is 'a bit of a nonsense, but don't tell the others that! I always loved the tradition and class of the ballroom.

'My favourite dance is the foxtrot. It's a proper dance with proper music. It has class. In the Latin, I can't possibly choose between the paso doble and the rumba, they are both such passionate, strong dances.'

ANTON DU BEKE

'Laila did really well,' he comments. 'She's one of the best stayers I've ever had, I'll give her that. I've been lucky with the girls I've danced with. They've all been lovely to be with. I had a fun time doing *Strictly* last year and long may it continue.

'Anyway, what would *Strictly* do without me? It would be half a show, wouldn't it!'

Despite his clowning and the constant stream of daft jokes, Anton warns that he's no pushover in the training room. But he is careful not to upset his celebrity dance partner.

'I can be quite firm,' he confirms. 'There are certain requirements I must have when we're in the studio but other than that I try and make it enjoyable because

Anton also studied ballet as a teenager to help him with his posture and found he had an innate talent. 'I have a natural turn out and a good jump so I was good at ballet.' He even auditioned for full-time dance schools but money was tight so he took a job as a baker, working from 3 a.m., and practising dance in his spare time.

The hilarious hoofer doesn't ask much from his celebrity dance partner, only that she has seen the show and understands the work involved. He is looking forward to pulling on his dancing shoes for series 8. 'I hope to have a great experience, have a fabulous partner and, essentially, I hope to have lots of fun.'

ango queen Flavia Cacace had her greatest success on *Strictly* when she was paired with *EastEnders* star Matt Di Angelo, who came second in series 5. 'What surprised me the most about Matt is how incredibly hard he tried. Matt was genuinely devastated when things went wrong, and that happened a few times. He put himself under pressure to do well for me. Making the final made me as happy as if we'd won.'

The year after she was out in the first week with Matt's former co-star Phil Daniels, and in the last season she was partnered with Craig Kelly, who scraped through on the public vote, despite several maulings from the judges, to dance in his home town of Blackpool. The dream ended after a cha-cha-cha that left the judges cold and reminded Craig Revel Horwood of 'a Thunderbird.'

After a long line of actors, Flavia says her ideal celeb would be a sportsman. 'Their stamina and determination would make a welcome change for

with my partner, but my parents were so supportive. I really couldn't have done it without them as they supported me both financially and mentally.'

Flavia met fellow Italian Vincent Simone who shared her dance teacher at the local studio. 'We had a try-out with each other and it worked perfectly,' says Flavia. 'It's a complete coincidence that we are both from Italy, but we met in the UK.'

THE DANCERS

me in the training room,' she explains. 'If I absolutely have to be partnered with David Beckham, I'll take it!'

When she was four, Naples-born Flavia moved to Guildford in Surrey with her large family. She had taken ballet lessons in Italy but took up ballroom dancing at six years old because her parents were unable to find a local ballet school. After winning several junior medals, a teacher suggested Flavia take part in competitions and, at twelve, she found a dance partner and started on the Sunday circuits. 'Mum and Dad spent so long taxiing me around to rehearse with my partner who lived miles away from where we lived,' she said. 'It was quite hard having to travel such long distances to practise

In 2001, the pair decided to turn professional, bagging several championship titles in Argentine tango, Ten-Dance and Show Dance. They also turned their talents to teaching at Danceworld, the dance school in Guildford where they met.

Since the show last year Flavia has been busy touring the nation with the *Strictly Professional Tour*. 'Physically, it is one of the hardest things I have ever done. Doing eighty-nine performances was exhausting!'

The 31-year-old dancer always looks forward to a new series of *Strictly* but this year she's particularly excited about her fellow professionals because 'the new boys are gorgeous!'

Last year, the Italian Stallion had a feisty partner in EastEnder Natalie Cassidy. Her fancy footwork and huge popularity with the public got the couple to week 11. 'Natalie was a really big personality,' he recalls. 'We were like best friends on the dance floor. We were just having so much fun!'

The tiny tango champ was born in Foggia, on the southern coast of Italy, into a family of dancers. With parents who are both teachers in ballroom and Latin he insists 'My dance career was bound to happen as dancing is such a massive part of Italian life. I remember that I would dance at any party that we went to; at aged five, I would be the one on the dance floor dancing around – my mother said I was born to perform.'

A dance tutor who originated from Milan soon recognised Vincent's talent and began to give him private lessons. He competed in his first competition in Rome at the age of nine and he and his partner came first out of seventy couples. At ten they were

His parents opened their own dance school when Vincent was twelve and he began to help out. 'I was fairly young to start teaching but I loved it. By the age of fourteen, some of the couples that I taught were the Italian and Regional Champions, and I was so proud of them and what we had achieved together.

'I knew that the dance capital of the world is London, and I realised if I wanted to make it professionally, I needed to come to England,' he says. 'So at seventeen I arrived in Surrey and found Flavia.'

Flavia and Vincent joined *Strictly* in series 4, when Vincent was paired with another EastEnder, Louisa Lytton, and reached the quarter-final.

'My first time on *Strictly* I was extremely lucky to be paired up with Louisa as she was probably one of the most talented celebrities ever to have taken part in *Strictly*,' he says.

'We had so much fun during the training sessions as I believe that having fun is the best way to learn to dance! She surprised me every Saturday with her performance, always giving it one hundred per cent.'

VINCENT SIMONE

The next series saw him partner Stephanie Beacham and, sadly, only make it to the second show. 'What can I say? Stephanie was a true diva. She is the one and only,' he admits.

In 2008, his partnership with Rachel Stevens saw him come closest to winning, just missing out in the final due to a spectacular show dance by Tom Chambers and Camilla Dallerup.

Vincent will be happy with any celebrity as long as she has passion – something he has plenty of. 'I will be able to teach anyone to dance and we will definitely get along with each other,' he says. 'I think people realise straightaway that I am easy to get along with and am an outrageous flirt, so watch out!'

Juvenile Italian Champions, a feat he repeated with a different partner every year from the age of twelve until he was fifteen.

BEHIND THE SCENES
Needles and Threads

Erin and Katya try on their bespoke waltz dresses ready for the group dance

Many of the Strictly dresses are carefully created from scratch by the team of seamstresses

Ian practises the routine backstage as Brendan's bow-tie is expertly tied moments before they are due on stage

Ali's tango dress gets some final alterations

The celebs may be the stars of the show but where would they be without the silk, satin and lace – and, in Ola's case, tiny bits of string – that make up the fabulous costumes?

While most of the dresses are ready to go by Saturday morning, the wardrobe department backstage is still a hive of activity right up until the start of the show, with plenty of last-minute panics and alterations.

'I arrive about 8 a.m. when it's quiet and I check around to make sure I have everything I need for the day,' says assistant wardrobe designer Nadia

Nigoumi. 'The team arrive around ten, then it's heads down for sewing on of bits and bobs, last-minute fittings, picking out earrings, all sorts of things. The mike leads arrive in the morning and we stitch them all in and put in pouches to receive the actual mike packs. When all that's done everyone starts steaming and pressing the clothes.

Head designer Su Judd works with the team during the week to get all the outfits ready, but on Saturday Nadia is in charge of the surprisingly tiny dressing room. Against one wall is a rail with an array of stunning dresses. As well as Ali Bastian's red-and-black tango outfit and Laila's deep blue American smooth gown, there are white and champagne-coloured ballroom dresses and a few of the male dancers' white shirts, as well as cycling shorts to stop their trousers riding up when they dance.

On the counter opposite, Jo from dancewear firm Chrisanne is gluing individual stones to the collars of shirts.

The male celebs' and dancers' suits are all steamed and pressed by the team to ensure they look immaculate on camera

'Today the dress rehearsal starts at two forty-five and we start dressing for that at two o'clock. I watch this final run-through to find out if anything needs tweaking or changing, and we sort out any accidents, like a heel getting caught in the hem of a dress. When it's over we have an hour or two before the live performance and sometimes we have to restitch the hems, so there's a real panic right up until the last minute.'

Costume secret: each shirt has a pair of cycling shorts sewn on to the bottom so the shirts can't come out of the trousers during the dance

DRESSING TIMES TX12	DRESS TIME	DRESSER	Dressing Room	Runner
			126	
			127	Medea
			128	
Bruno			125	
Craig			2	Will
Darcey			3	Micky
Len	14.00	Sarah	205	Tim
Aliona	14.15 14.30	Sue	1	Will
Erin	14.30	Sue	4	Micky
Flavia	14.00	Sarah	217	Chloe
Katya	14.30	Lisa	211	Gaby
Kristina	14.30	Lena	29	Gaby
Natalie L	14.15	Lena	28	Chloe
Ola	14.15 14.30	Lisa	130	Chloe
Ali	14.15	Sarah	130	Will
Laila	14.30	Billy		Gaby

With so many fittings to get through before the dress rehearsal begins, a schedule is crucial

The costume team have to be highly organised – in the changing room, all the costumes are arranged and labelled by dancer or celeb name

Each dress is planned out with a design spec before it is made, and the colour and shape requirements are tailored to each dancer or celebrity

Each shirt is painstakingly decorated by hand with sparkling rhinestones

'We have five boys in the professional dance tonight and we had three shirts already stoned up from two series ago so we've had to get two more shirts for James and Vincent and stone them up,' explains Nadia. 'Jo's already done one shirt today and now she's on the second.'

It's not uncommon for dresses and shirts to be recycled for the professionals or even for the celebrities.

'Sometimes dresses will pop up again because they take so long to make. If the powers that be slot in an extra dance, which they very often do, Su can't get someone to make them in time – it's not physically possible – so she might take outfits from the last series or from the tour.

'We have some dresses today that were on the tour and we'll have some next week too, for the professionals who wore them. Su doesn't often do it for individual dances, because they are made specially, but for group dances she might.'

Many of the more stunning outfits can't be used again, however, because they have been sold on to private buyers. The dresses are on loan from Chrisanne and another company called DSI and on Monday morning they are returned to be sold on.

'People ring up from all over the world and say, "I want the dress that Ola wore or Erin wore,"' Nadia

reveals. 'Usually they are professional dancers or amateur dancers but they can just be fans. The outfits sometimes get damaged too, especially the men's satin shirts because satin is very delicate. If his partner is wearing lots of body make-up, for example, it comes off on the shirt and ruins it, and sequins and stones can rub against it.'

Although the planning for the wardrobe begins in August, the fittings are completed during the week of the show. And in some cases that can mean going right down to the wire. As Nadia and her team sew in microphones, Erin Boag comes in for a fitting of her American smooth outfit and the girls bustle around her with pins to mark final alterations.

'Su goes to visit the Chrisanne and DSI girls at their places of work and liaises with them about the outfits and that's also where all the celebs and pros go to have their fittings during the week. Sometimes we have the fittings here later because we can't get to them during the week. For example, Natalie Lowe is doing all her training in Liverpool because that's where Ricky is working, so we do her fittings on a Friday or Saturday.'

Each dress is built around a basic dance leotard, which looks like a sheer swimsuit, and the padding for the bra is sewn inside. For the bustier celebs, however, there needs to be a little more in the way of

The essential equipment backstage contrasts with the glitter and glitz on the dance floor.

Erin examines one of her costumes as she waits in her dressing room between performances

support. And when an ugly mike pack might ruin the line of a dress, sometimes it's put in the bosom of the dress by sewing in a little pouch. Even with Ola's skin tight catsuits and skimpy outfits, the mike has to go in the bosom.'

Nadia then explains that Ola's samba outfit, which covers very little of her body, took the longest to make this week because it is carefully constructed of so many tiny parts.

As well as making final changes to this week's outfits, Nadia already has one eye on next week's show. The professional dancers are frequently popping in to try on outfits for next week but the celeb dresses can't be finalised until the designers know who is staying in the competition.

'Su has a massive chart of who's wearing what when. Then as the series moves on and people leave, so dresses might not be made at all or the fabric might have been cut out already, in which case she might move things around.

'Last week Natalie Cassidy was knocked out but the dress she would have worn this week might go to somebody else for another dance because the colour or style is right. It's like a huge jigsaw puzzle in Su's head – I don't know how she does it.'

Her most famous roles have seen her knee-deep in mud, and a great deal worse. But the star of *The Good Life* and *Rosemary and Thyme* is looking forward to swapping the gardening gloves for a glamorous frock and shedload of sequins.

But she has a warning for her dance partner. 'I would say I am a slow learner but when I have got something then that's it,' she reveals. 'It just depends whether my dance partner will have the patience!'

Strictly won't result in murder on the dance floor.

'The only thing I am really worried about is going into the unknown,' she admits. 'I just hope I do well on the first few dances it would be such a shame if I fell over or got injured.'

And despite being one of the older contestants at 64, the sex symbol of the seventies is still keen to show the viewers a bit of hip action.

'There is no telling at the moment whether I will prefer ballroom or Latin,' she says. 'It's the

FELICITY KENDAL

The small-screen legend is no stranger to the spotlight, having made her stage debut at the age of nine months, when she was cast as a changeling baby in *A Midsummer Night's Dream*. At nineteen, she starred alongside father Geoffrey in the Merchant-Ivory film *Shakespeare Wallah*, which is loosely based on her own theatrical family and their life in India where she grew up. After returning to England to launch a stage career, Felicity starred in a series of plays in the West End before getting her big TV break in 1975 as Barbara in *The Good Life*. The sitcom, which also starred Richard Briers as a high-flying designer who chucks in his job to become self-sufficient, with Felicity as his long-suffering wife, was a massive hit and turned her into a star. It also gained her millions of male admirers and in 1981 she was the second-ever recipient of the Rear of the Year title.

After *The Good Life* ended in 1978, Felicity took the lead role in many more sitcoms including *The Mistress*, *Solo* and *Honey for Tea*. In more recent years, as well as a successful career on the stage, she has starred opposite Pam Ferris as a landscape gardener turned detective in *Rosemary and Thyme*. And while she's used to solving homicides in stately homes on a weekly basis, she's hoping joining

choreography and the speed of it that will be the problem, but I think I am rather keen on Latin, and it will be a dance I rather like. I fear the quickstep as it's not "showy"; you just have to be good at it technically. And the jive… Well, I think that's out of the question.'

Felicity is not a total stranger to dance and once tangoed with one of the most amazing dancers of all time.

'I do have a very small amount of dance experience. My claim to fame is the fact that I danced the tango in a film called *Valentino* with Rudolf Nureyev. Also my mother taught me to waltz when I was four years old. In fact, bizarrely, since I have signed up for the show I have found a letter that said that my mother always wanted to be a dancer. She danced a lot when she was younger, dancing the waltz and the foxtrot and was very good.

'The last time I danced properly was two years ago when I was in a Noël Coward play and I danced the foxtrot. But more recently it was at my son's twenty-first birthday party where I got drunk and danced the way I wanted to!'

The actress, who has two grown-up sons and two stepdaughters, is always keen to try new things –

she even got her first tattoo at the age of 63. So she jumped at the chance to dance on *Strictly*.

'When I was asked to take part in *Strictly* I found it impossible to refuse. The show is full of the right energy, it is such good fun, you get fit, and how many times do you get to dance with such fantastic professional dancers? I think the thing that is fun is that dancing is so different to acting for me. It's not my day job and so there is no pressure and I just think it's wonderful to try something new.'

And as long as she leaves the wellies at home, she'll definitely be one to watch.

Dancing WITH THE STARS

The format of *Strictly Come Dancing* has spread its glitter around the world with sister shows in over 30 countries. The biggest and glitziest of these is the US version, *Dancing With the Stars*, which has our own Len Goodman and Bruno Tonioli judging alongside choreographer Carrie Ann Inaba. Although it first kicked up its heels in 2005, it has already overtaken *Strictly* with ten seasons under its sparkly belt, as there are two a year.

All this keeps Len and Bruno very busy, especially in the autumn season, when they have to fly back every week for the British version.

'It is tiring,' Bruno admits. 'But this year, because the UK show starts two weeks later, we'll only be flying back and forth for eight weeks instead of ten.'

Because the rules are less stringent when it comes to lifts and holds, the dances tend to be more theatrical and less formal, which appeals to Bruno's showbiz side.

'It is a bit more showy because all the ballroom is done in an American smooth style so it's more glitzy and Hollywood. That's what they like in America and you have to give the public what they want. Here we do the classic version of the ballroom dances.'

As well as exporting the judges, *Strictly Come Dancing* has been known to import the odd dancer from the shows abroad, and Brian Fortuna joined in the sixth series of *Strictly* fresh from the Stateside version. He was struck by the similarities to the UK show.

'When I walked on to the set in London it felt almost identical,' Brian says. 'The US set is a little bit larger but you pretty much feel like you're in the same place.'

Autumn 2009 saw pop legend Donny Osmond succeed where sister Marie had failed, beating singer Mya to lift the trophy. The spring 2010 series saw Pussycat Doll Nicole Scherzinger and partner Derek Hough perform a purr-fect jive and Argentine tango to win, leaving figure skater Evan Lysacek in the cold.

Given Nicole's past career as a pop singer and dancer, some suggested she had an unfair advantage but both *Strictly* judges are quick to jump to her defence.

'What are you going to do? Are you going to stop people doing the show because they were in a band?' asks Bruno. 'We've had Mel B and Emma Bunton on *Strictly* and it's totally different doing ballroom and Latin to what you may do in a group. Having somebody that good actually brought everybody else's game up and, in fact, the last season of *Dancing With the Stars* was the best one ever. We had the highest viewing figures ever after ten series.'

Len believes Nicole had no more of a head start than the sports personalities that compete.

'I do understand that point of view but my answer is always that okay, she was in a pop group and she was maybe used to moving to music. She's probably been to stage school and done a bit of tap and jazz and modern and all these things, which of course is a help. But is it more of a help than Evan Lysacek, the ice dancer, who is a trained athlete?

'Sports people are used to being coached, they all have the will to win, far more than somebody on the stage has got, and their whole ethos is "when the going gets tough, the tough get going". So you could say sports people have an advantage.'

While many of the contestants are more famous Stateside than in the UK, there are plenty of familiar names in the two lists. Len and Bruno gave us their verdict on a selected few.

Season 9

Donny Osmond
Winner

Len: 'Marie was in it before but Donny is the better dancer. Even so, for me and the other judges, the singer Mya, who was runner-up, should have won it. It was a bit like Ricky and Chris in the *Strictly* final. The best dancer ended up as runner-up because the other one was more popular with viewers. Donny won it because he's a legend. There's not a soul in America, or probably in Britain, that doesn't like him.'

Bruno: 'I've known Donny for years because I used to work with him as a choreographer in the eighties and he is one of the most professional, nicest guys in the industry. He is incredible, such a hard worker. I don't think there's anyone in the industry who could say anything bad about him.'

Kelly Osbourne
Third place

Len: 'The one who was the absolute surprise package was Kelly Osbourne. She was brilliant and she got through the semi-final and came third, deservedly. Like a few of them she had the odd dodgy moment in the series but overall, the wild child became the mild child. She really went for it. You see this young girl come out, covered in

tattoos, Ozzy Osbourne's daughter, and she really went for it. You could tell she was trying her hardest throughout and she was very good.'

Melissa Joan Hart
Eliminated seventh

Len: 'Melissa Joan Hart, from *Sabrina the Teenage Witch*, was all right. She did one wonderful dance, funnily enough the Charleston, which was outstanding, but the rest of her dances were average.'

Ashley Hamilton
First out

Len: 'Ashley Hamilton is George Hamilton's son and George, when he was on, realised straightaway that he couldn't dance so he went for the comedy and the fun of it, and came out in the paso dressed as Zorro. Ashley was really wooden and probably deserved to be the first to go!'

Season 10

Nicole Scherzinger
Winner

Len: 'Nicole was, without doubt, the best there's ever been on any of the series I've judged. She was truly incredible. I think it helped that she had Derek as her professional because he is a genius. I've never said that about any of them, but Derek Hough's choreography is genius. That boy is brilliant.'

Bruno: 'Nicole is a lovely girl, very nice, and was dancing with lovely Derek. They were very hardworking. They really deserved to win, there's no question.'

Pamela Anderson
Eliminated seventh

Len: 'What I loved about Pamela Anderson is that she embraced the competition fully. She didn't just take the money, get kicked off and go, she really embraced it and whatever dance she did, she was in character. She was a bit like Barry Humphries. As soon as he gets in the clothes he becomes Dame Edna. Pamela Anderson was like that. If she was doing an American smooth-style foxtrot, she was Marilyn Monroe for the whole day. She never changed that persona – she was that character. She was a genius at that. I was so impressed with her as far as that's concerned. For me, she went a bit early. She was in the dance off in the first week so to carry on as far as she did, I thought, was outstanding.'

Bruno: 'Pamela Anderson was gorgeous – a good dancer and a great performer.'

Kate Gosselin
Eliminated fourth

Len: 'Kate was the most famous one in America, and the reason they got such huge figures. She starred in a reality show with her husband and eight kids and she's massive so she was on the front pages of everything, but she wasn't a great dancer.'

Buzz Aldrin
Eliminated second

Len: 'Buzz should have been first but he is truly a legend. I was expecting a John Sergeant moment there, with him keeping on coming back, but fortunately he only lasted a couple of weeks. He was how you would imagine an eighty-three-year-old astronaut would dance – what was on the label was in the tin. Good luck to him for having a go, but he was very difficult to critique because I have such respect for this man. We were all a bit on eggshells because he's an absolute legend and one of the first guys on the moon.'

Bruno: 'Buzz Aldrin wasn't so much dancing as just appearing. But it was wonderful to meet him and his very lovely wife.'

DANCING WITH THE STARS

45

I f anyone can bring some extra magic to the dance floor, it's Paul Daniels. And it seems the talented magician has a back-up plan in case the dancing doesn't come naturally.

'There use to be a Penny Spencer formation team on *Come Dancing* and they had magic cabinets on stage and made their partners appear,' he recalls. 'So maybe if I don't pick up the dancing I can impress everyone doing that.'

The Middlesbrough-born son of a cinema

'I have absolutely no dance experience,' he reveals. 'In fact, I am totally the wrong size and shape to be a dancer and am not elegant at all. I have no idea if I can dance but I guess I am about to find out.

'According to my dad if someone else can do something and they have the same number of hands and feet as you, then you can do it too.

'Debbie is a brilliant dancer but she was trained by the Royal Ballet not ballroom. Debbie and I don't ballroom dance. At weddings and functions about all

PAUL DANIELS

projectionist, Paul's interest in magic was awakened at eleven when he read a book on party entertaining. He began to practise magic tricks as a hobby and, after completing his National Service, he worked in his parents' grocery store by day and played the working men's clubs at night.

After buying his own mobile grocery business, Paul was offered a summer season at Newquay in 1969, and he sold up to concentrate on his act. A year later he appeared on *Opportunity Knocks* and came second, but he caught the eye of TV producer Johnnie Hamp who gave him a regular slot on Granada's *The Wheeltappers and Shunters Social Club* hosted by Bernard Manning. In 1979, he landed his own series on the BBC and the *The Paul Daniels Magic Show* began its fifteen-year run.

While not performing, Paul has worked his magic behind the scenes, designing special effects for stage and screen on such productions as *Cats*, *Phantom of the Opera* and the film *Return to Oz*. He was also commissioned by the English National Ballet to create magical effects for *The Nutcracker*.

Wife Debbie McGee, who first met him when she auditioned to be his 'glamorous assistant', is a trained dancer but Paul is not sure he'll be a natural.

I can manage is to hold Debbie close and move the upper part of my body as I simply don't know what else to do.'

Although at 72 he is the most senior contestant on this series, Paul is adamant that you can teach an old dog new tricks.

'One of my mottos in life is you should not go to bed without learning something new every day,' he says. 'I just like having fun and yes it would be great to win but I would be happy for whoever wins and am just looking forward to enjoying the journey.

'I have no fears about actually taking part in the show but I just hope at the end of it I can dance and that I can add it to my list of things I can do.'

When it comes to criticism from the judges, Paul says he will like it – not a lot!

'It depends if I respect where it comes from,' he reasons. 'You need to look at the criticism and see if it is constructive or destructive and make a note of it if it's constructive but if it's destructive simply disregard it.

'I just like having fun. When you can't do something you can only get better. I will just have a go. This is not my career, this is fun.'

No doubt our TV magician has a few tricks up his sleeve.

alesha
unleashed

Former *Strictly Come Dancing* champ Alesha Dixon added an extra element of glamour to the judging panel in series 7 and brought a different perspective to the comments. Drawing from her experience as a contestant, the singer saw not just the dance but also the long hours of training, the dedication and the problems with each move that had gone before it.

But her debut on the panel, in September 2009, was not without its controversy as she was replacing original judge Arlene Phillips.

'It was hard last year because there was a lot of negativity before I had even started,' she admits. 'But I am a fighter and I was determined not to let any of the negative opinions get to me. I hope people can move on now as the focus should be on the contestants, not me. They are, after all, the ones doing *Strictly*.'

Having taken the plunge, as a judge Alesha soon carved a niche for herself by empathising with the struggle of the less talented dancers and with every bump and bruise the contestants suffered. She also had an eye for glamour, at one point calling Jade and Ian 'best-dressed couple of the evening' and delighting in Ricky Groves' week one outfit with, 'He's wearing pink. He should get points for wearing pink. I love a man in pink.'

This year, Alesha is returning as an established part of the show and she can't wait to get back behind the judges' table.

'I'm really excited,' she says. 'I am really looking forward to the new set, pro dancers and sitting in the judges' chairs with the boys. I have the best seat in the house. I am also looking forward to seeing how the contestants get on and who will shine.

'And of course I can't wait to put on some sparkly dresses!'

alesha tells all

What kind of judge are you?

I want to be myself and be as honest as I can. I respect the show and what it is all about and I want to see the same from the contestants. It's important to be helpful and give people advice so they can work on things.

Are you more confident this year?

I am just very relaxed. I was quite relaxed last year, but to everyone else it probably appeared quite stressful. The truth is I really enjoyed myself last year and I am raring to go this year.

What advice would you give to the contestants?

Embrace the moment, listen to the judges and just enjoy it. Try not to let the nerves get to you. Going on *Strictly* is such an amazing opportunity.

Do you enjoy working with the other judges?

Yes, all of them are so lovely and Bruno is such a laugh. He is so full of energy. I feel it is such an honour to be asked to judge the show and it's a joy to be part of it.

Who are you looking forward to watching?

Goldie. He is going to surprise loads of people. He is a lot of fun and he will bring great entertainment to the show. I am also looking forward to watching Ann Widdecombe because she is so strongly opinionated.

Who would be your dream contestant?

Lily Allen. She is a nice girl and she is a fan of the show, so she would be great to watch.

Which is more nerve-racking — being a judge on Strictly or performing as a pop star on stage?

Performing on stage, without a doubt. Performing to a crowded audience is always nerve-racking.

Which male judge is the most flamboyant?

Craig is the most flamboyant in his style. He will come in and wear really wacky things, which I love.

Do you think the judges overstep the mark?

No, we are completely in our rights to say what we think. When Brucie and Brendan had a pop at Craig last year, he was perfectly in his rights to say what he said. I enjoyed watching Brendan's reaction though. Strictly is an entertainment programme and people should not take it too seriously. When the show's over it's all forgotten and we have a laugh and a drink in the bar. We all get on so well, just like a big family.

STRICTLY *style*

Long before the celebrities get near the dance floor, *Strictly* designer Su Judd is collecting ideas and beavering away at designs for the new series. More than a month before the opening show, work begins in earnest and Su comes up with a huge complicated chart detailing what each couple will be wearing for the whole series, and one of the first engagements for each celeb is a measuring and discussion session with Su and her team.

When the ideas that Su and the other designers come up with have been realised and everything is ready for each show, Su takes a step back and hands over to Nadia Nigoumi, who runs the wardrobe department during the frenzy of the actual live programme.

'I am the person who goes round saying "I'd really like this to be blue" but Nadia has to organise all the dressers and keep all the celebrities under control when they're all terrified. She's brilliant,' reveals Su.

'The team backstage on the night are very experienced dressers, many of whom have worked in opera and ballet where thirty-second changes happen every night, and they are all specialists. We have some that come in and sew and some who are professional dressers and Nadia has to run the tightest ship. It's quite hectic on Saturday night.'

Despite the scrupulous attention to detail, however, every series includes a wardrobe malfunction or two. In series 7, Jade popped out of a dress, a float from Zoe's wrist came off and got tangled around James's feet, and a couple of contestants trod on dresses.

'Jade's foot got caught in her dress during the foxtrot,' recalls the stylist. 'Actually, she'd been telling us all day it was too long and we had taken it up once, then she got it caught in the lining. With all the dances you can only go with what happens in the run-through.

'This year, the costumes are going to be more theatrical than usual, so there might be more of these incidents – although I hope not.'

Malfunctions aside, the show would never be the same without the glitter, sparkle and flesh-flashing that the costume department provides.

Looking back on series 7, Su gave us the rundown of her favourite outfits – and dished the dirt on the celebrity dancers.

Ali's Silver and White Waltz Dress

This white dress with silver straps coming down from the shoulder was fabulous. It was designed by Vicky Barkess, who works for DSI [a dancewear firm], and she was keen to use Ali as a muse because she has that great figure, those great legs and an elegant look. Before we even knew she could dance we saw her as a fabulous model. Persuading any of the celebrities to wear shoulder pads was really hard because when they put their arms up, the pads can get in their way and the dancers hate it. In fact, Brian detested that dress. He's a very classic boy and the

shoulder pads were a bit too punky and funky for him. He wanted Ali to look very simple and elegant, but I think the dress is a real stunner.

Ali was easy to dress and a lovely girl. As the series went on though, and she became more involved with Brian, she had her own ideas and wanted to go for more simplicity because she learnt more about dancing and understood the fact that essentially a ballroom gown is more sports gear than a fashion item. We were trying to push the boundaries but she was learning to dance and she loved it.

Jade's Red Salsa Dress

This dress had 30 metres of frill although it was actually longer to start with, and we cut some off. We also added Mark Foster's paso doble belt from the previous series. Before that it had been part of Matt di Angelo's salsa outfit, then it was Mark Foster's and then it was sewn into Jade's dress. Because she is so tall we had to make virtually everything from scratch. As she is very sports minded, and used to sportswear fitting exactly to allow her to do strenuous things, everything had to be perfect. She asked for a lot of alterations, even on the day of the show.

It was all about mental power and winning attitude. However, if she loved a dress and she wanted to wear it, that was enough for her. She fitted into a pale yellow dress of Kristina's for the foxtrot and because she loved it so much she was prepared to put up with it being a tight fit. Kristina is tiny so Jade wore it through sheer force of will!

We had to cut the pants out of the leotard and make that because she is so long and lean, and we put a six-inch strip along the bottom to get the length of it right.

Zoe's Electric-Blue Jive Dress

Zoe was terrified of showing anything so that was actually a very covered-up dress, although it doesn't seem like that to most people. We had to put a lot of netting in the body and bring it high up the back but I think she looked really cute. She's a huge Dusty Springfield fan and this was her Dusty moment. One of the make-up ladies, who had worked with Dusty, gave Zoe a pair of her false eyelashes. When she got in that dress and her make-up was done, we told her she really looked like Dusty and that she should wear the Dusty eyelashes but Zoe said, 'No, I'm never wearing them. I'm putting them in a frame.'

The big thing with Zoe was that she always had to have a neckband because when I first met her I showed her a picture of Sophia Loren, whom I initially based all her looks on, and she had chiffon around her neck. From then on that was what she felt she needed every time she danced. Zoe had this terrible fear of going out and mucking up so the neckband became her security blanket. The jive was the one outfit when she didn't wear it and she got one of her lowest marks, so she said, 'Don't ever let me go out there without something round my neck again.' All her dresses were designed with that in mind.

Laila's Paso Doble Dress

For the paso we wanted to give Laila a Frida Kahlo look – we even wanted to fill in her eyebrows but that didn't go down well with Laila! The dance was in Blackpool and I got to watch that from the gods, where the lighting was set up. It looked amazing and that dress really wanted to be filmed from the top, because that see-through skirt, as Anton threw her around, was incredibly effective, very dramatic and really fitting for the bigger venue of Blackpool. The body was similar to Zoe's jive dress, with the cut-outs that defined the curves filled in with net, and a good idea like that often re-emerges for another outfit.

Natalie Cassidy's Purple Jive Dress

Every single one of Natalie Cassidy's dresses sold out instantly because she has an average-sized figure so more people can fit into her clothes.

Out of everyone, Natalie was the easiest to work with because as an actress she's used to being put into outfits. She knew her limitations and absolutely loved dressing up. Her favourite dress was the purple jive one with the skirt that sticks out. It was at the time when Lady Gaga was hitting the big time and we called that her Gaga dress, because it was loosely based on what Gaga wore in Glastonbury.

Ricky Groves' Jive Jacket with New York Skyline

This jacket had the New York skyline in stones on the front and was a good test for this year because that's the way we plan to go for series 8 – more theatrical and showy. We made similar jackets for Chris Parker in the first series and, like him, Ricky was such a personality that he needed something a little bit lively. The jacket was so expensive to make that we had to stop stoning the back, which is why the skyline at the back is one line. All the money went on the front! We used a cheaper crystal for this but there are still £300 worth of stones on the jacket, glued on individually.

Ricky loved that jacket and it was auctioned off for Children in Need so the money went to a good cause.

Ricky Whittle's Paso Doble Outfit

Ricky was really fantastic on every count. He is a lovely man, really at ease with what he's doing, not at all precious or vain. He was so easy for me to dress. He was compliant with everything we did so we made him wear fluorescent pink for his first Latin dance!

My favourite outfit was his paso, where he wore very high-waisted trousers that went up into his ribcage and laced up at the front. They were very high at the back and the satin blouse came out at the shoulder-blades then came in to show the curves of the back.

They had belonged to Brendan in series 2, when he wore them with the bare-chested jacket. They look so much better on Ricky Whittle because he has the hipbones and the bottom (sorry, Brendan!). Whereas Brendan is wide and slim, Ricky is more solid and is leaner as you look at him front on, so they fitted so beautifully. We didn't even have to alter them because they were laced up at the crutch so you could adjust them easily.

Annoyingly for the public, when I first met Ricky I thought, 'We could have him near-naked every week but that would be too easy.' I think people would have expected that. Sorry, girls.

Actress and mum Patsy is as well known for her personal life as her screen roles, counting Liam Gallagher and Simple Minds frontman Jim Kerr among her ex-husbands. Recently divorced from DJ Jeremy Healy, Patsy decided to take part in *Strictly* to gain a much-needed boost.

'I have had a pretty bad year personally and they say dance lifts your spirits,' she says. 'And I am excited about the challenge.

because the long commute meant little time with her sons, she joined *Holby City* as ward sister Faye Morton.

Describing herself primarily as a mum, she feels she may prefer to stick to the more sedate dances – for the sake of her boys.

'I am a mum and see myself very much as that, so I think ballroom is very elegant and I guess more appropriate,' she explains. 'I fear all the Latin dances. I just don't want to embarrass the kids. I want to be appropriate but I guess I have got to let go of the fear.

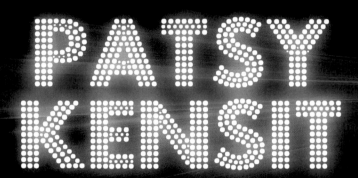

PATSY KENSIT

'The fitness side also appeals to me. I have not danced since I was sixteen and although I exercise every day in the gym, I am interested in putting my body through something different and it will hopefully give me a new lease of life.'

Patsy grew up in the East End as the daughter of a gangster, who she believed was an antiques dealer. At eighteen months of age, her mother signed her up to a theatrical agency and she found fame at four, as the little girl who popped her cheek in the iconic ad for frozen peas. Her first film role was in the British comedy *For the Love of Ada* and at six, she played Mia Farrow's daughter in *The Great Gatsby*. Two years later she also appeared in *The Blue Bird* with Elizabeth Taylor.

At eighteen, Patsy launched her adult film career with the lead in *Absolute Beginners* and also started a career in pop as the singer in the band Eighth Wonder, with brother Jamie on guitar. They had a huge hit with 'I'm Not Scared' before Patsy returned to her acting career starring opposite Mel Gibson in *Lethal Weapon 2*.

After the split from the Oasis frontman she relaunched her career with a role as superbitch Sadie King in *Emmerdale* and, after leaving the show

'If I do Latin it might tap into a "me" that has lain dormant. I am however really looking forward to doing the tango as I love the story. To be honest, I am just really eager to learn.'

Despite being a Londoner through and through, Patsy is most excited about going 'up north' to dance in the home of ballroom.

'Of course I would love to win but I am not sure I will,' she says. 'My dream is to dance at Blackpool as I love the north and I would love to dance in front of a northern audience. That's the dream, but I could be booted out in the first week.'

As a huge fan of *Come Dancing* as a child, the 42-year-old star is thrilled to be given the opportunity to strut her stuff and says she hasn't done any choreographed dancing since *Absolute Beginners*.

'I hope this experience is a journey. I love the show, I am a huge fan of the show and I am here to surrender to the experience,' she says.

'I used to watch *Come Dancing* when I was younger and I found it fascinating. I even had a doll with a *Come Dancing*-style dress. The whole thing is a process, its not just about learning a few steps, and I am really open to it. I just hope I don't humiliate my kids and that the boys are proud of me.'

Ready, Set, Glow

Strictly Come Dancing burst on to our screens in 2004 in an explosion of red and gold, and the iconic set has remained much the same ever since, until this year when the producers decided it was time for a makeover. Cue Patrick Doherty, the creator of the original design and the perfect pair of hands to remodel the *Strictly* set without losing any of its sumptuous charm.

The talented production designer had plenty of ideas to bring the show up to date.

'It's a complete reinvention of the same set,' he explains. 'What we've tried to do is keep the essence of what is *Strictly*, but completely update the set so it feels fresh, more exciting and more vibrant. We've lost the gold and red theme of the audience environment and we've put in new light boxes, which are metal with silver glitter, so we've gone for a more silver and purple feel. However, we still have the red drapes at the back of the set because they were the lynchpin of the whole thing.'

After seven series of lurking in her boudoir behind the stage, Tess has now been elevated to the giddy heights of a balcony within the main studio.

'Tess's area is all purple and silver and is now in the foreground of the studio,' says Patrick. 'We have two staircases downstage that lead you up to the two audience balconies, one of which is now Tess's area, so after the dance the couples go up the staircase to chat to Tess, who looks down over the whole set.'

In order to gain more areas for the dancers to perform, a raised middle platform has been built above the band, with staircases leading down onto the main floor as before. This is also where the competing couples make their entrance at the start of the show.

'Four staircases coming down into the set means you have more performance area,' reveals Patrick. 'So there is a possibility that they could start a dance in Tess's area and arrive down at the dance floor if they wanted to.'

The biggest and most spectacular change is the ability to project images across the entire set, achieved by special screens placed in the walls, floor and even the stairs.

'At the back is a screen, with two half-circular cross arches in front, all of which are full of LED screens so we can run a

projected image on the floor, up the staircases, which also house screens, up into the area of the main stage and up into the arches. So the whole back wall of the set is now a canvas and we can change the look and feel of the show at the touch of a button.

'At the launch show the pro dancers performed to 'Live And Let Die', and we projected big explosions on to the backdrop with the fire running through the set and up into the wall. It was pretty spectacular.'

Another fantastic innovation is the flying rig, which means the professional routines can literally start in the air.

'In the first launch show we used a vertical flight, where we bring the dancers down from the upper area so it's static. But we are hoping to have a moving flying rig where the dancers can fly out around the audience and back down again, probably starting at our new raised performance stage above the band and dropping down to the dance floor.'

While the dimensions of the 14 x 9 metre dance floor remain the same, the technology behind its assembly has moved on.

'We have 150 sections of dance floor of which we use 130, so that we have twenty spare,' says Patrick. 'It is a special sprung floor from America which clicks together and it's very low. The original dance floor had a steel frame that needed to be constructed before we laid our floor on top, but this is much quicker because the whole unit is already sprung, which gives the dancers the movement they require.'

Patrick began work on the new design in March and, by the time all the details had been ironed out,

had just six weeks to get the various components of the set built. As the whole thing has to be dismantled after the show and rebuilt each week, the production staff has to get the operation down to a fine art.

'For the initial build we had a week and a half because everything comes down in bits and gets assembled,' he says. 'There were in excess of ten different build contractors to get the set built, which is *very* unusual. A lot of that is to do with the new technology because we had screen companies and LED specialists to help us set up for the first time.

'The next time we went in it was cut down to about four days, with a team of twelve people, because everything had been assembled. When the show goes week-to-week live, we have two days and we have double crews, so we can work through the night.'

Although viewers will notice a big difference, Patrick has been careful to ensure they will be comfortable with the new look.

'We've done away with the Victorian theme in favour of a much more thirties feel, so it looks like a dynamic thirties ballroom.

'When we did the original series eight years ago, it was two small arches with some steel decking for the audience, a fan at the back where the band were and two staircases. It now feels like you're in a much bigger environment, more like Blackpool. The audience size has gone up to nearly 700 from 525, which is as many as we can manage with the dance floor in the middle, and it's really moved to become something more contemporary. The key was to ensure that when you turn on the TV, you know exactly what programme you're watching. I hope we've achieved that, but in a really exciting way.'

58

THE LIVE TOUR

Whatever the result of a *Strictly* series, the Live Tour can turn it on its head. The 2010 season saw Austin Healey, who failed to make it into the semis on the show, finally triumph in the arena. It was battle of the bulge as the muscle-bound rugby hero split the vote with the equally beefy Mark Ramprakash, and claimed victory at 23 shows to the cricketer's 20. Ali Bastian and partner Brian Fortuna snatched away just two triumphs and the rest of the couples, including current champs Chris and Ola, were left with nothing.

Ali and Chris were joined by fellow series 7 contestants Zoe Lucker, reunited with James Jordan, Ricky Groves, paired with Aliona Vilani, and Natalie Cassidy, who swapped dance partner Vincent for Darren Bennett. Kelly Brook, who dropped out of series 5 after a family bereavement, was given another chance to impress the judges when she returned with new dance partner Matthew Cutler. And impress she did.

'Kelly Brook was a fantastic dancer and came out on top every time,' reveals Craig. 'She was dancing with Matt for the first time and it was a good combination that got better and better with each show. But people didn't vote for her – she didn't win once.'

For once, the judges all agree, with Bruno confirming, 'Kelly is a stunning, fantastic dancer', and Len admitting she was top of his list.

'Kelly Brook was great and she was lovely,' he says. 'She never won it but she did as far as the judges were concerned, several times. She danced a fantastic jive and a fantastic foxtrot. She was top notch. But a lot of the audience are women so maybe there's a touch of jealousy in the voting.'

Apart from Kelly, however, Len chose Mark, dancing with Kristina Rihanoff, and Austin, who swapped Erin Boag for the lovely Lilia Kopylova.

'Kelly was great, Austin Healey was fantastic and Mark Ramprakash was brilliant. They were my top three.'

Unlike the TV show, the *Strictly* tour, with 45 performances in ten different cities, sees the couple repeat the same two dances every night. This results in an inevitable improvement in the standard.

'By the time we get to the end of the tour they're all getting too good,' explains Bruno. 'They get better and better. Austin and Mark Ramprakash were particularly good but Chris was great and Ali danced like a dream. They were such a great company. Apart from what they did in the show, just being away with them was such fun. It was a really good team.'

EastEnder and natural-born entertainer Ricky

> *'The huge venues can mean logistical headaches for everyone from the professional dancers, who have to rejig their routines to cover a floor four times bigger than usual, to the costume department, who have to deal with dresses worn every night. '*

Groves, however, bucked the trend when he changed one of his routines halfway through.

'Ricky was terrible to begin with,' recalls Craig. 'Then he had a shock to find he was the butt of every joke and he started improving. They suddenly changed his Viennese waltz to an American smooth, which he did to "Chim Chim Cher-ee" and it was much better because it was entertaining.

'Austin Healey won a lot and the audience loved him. Mark Ramprakash brought along that divine salsa, which was brilliant.'

Reigning champ Chris Hollins grabbed at the chance to reunite Team Cola, even though it meant travelling around the country after doing his morning shift on breakfast TV.

'I loved the tour. It was great to spend more time dancing with Ola and it was great to see past champions as well, like Ramps.

'Also, we got to meet the people who had voted for us face to face, because most of them can't see it at the BBC studio. It was also lovely to talk to all the kids who loved our dancing, and meet some of the Cola fans.'

The three male judges were reunited with former colleague Arlene Phillips for the tour and the audience were delighted to see her.

'It was great to have Arlene on tour and the crowd gave her rapturous applause,' says Craig. 'She was on top form.'

The five-week spectacular, which gives die-hard Strictly fans a chance to see their favourite couples perform live, relies on a portable set that includes a dance floor made up of 1200 panels, which can be put together to make a space of up to 900 square metres. A fleet of lorries, including a whole truck for costumes alone, ferries the necessary equipment to venues from London to Glasgow, and the celebrities and dancers follow in two buses.

The huge venues can mean logistical headaches for everyone from the professional dancers, who have to rejig their routines to cover a floor four times bigger than usual, to the costume department, who have to deal with dresses worn every night. Each outfit is sprayed and put in a hot box after wear and, if cleaning is needed, they are literally wiped down with baby wipes.

Despite the difficulties of getting the *Strictly* show from the studio on to the road, Bruno says that you can't beat the immediacy of a huge live audience.

'When you have ten thousand people watching and joining in it is incredible, really great fun,' he gushes. 'You have the real fans watching the show, it's a fabulous spectacle and there's such energy.'

Bubbly Ola had the time of her life with Chris Hollins and, as the icing on the cake, emerged as *Strictly* champion.

'Winning *Strictly* was the best achievement ever, in my life,' she gushes. 'It was an unbelievable moment. To be able to go all the way to the final with Chris, a friend and someone who has never danced before, was such an achievement.' And the proud Polish professional keeps her glitterball on the bedside table, to taunt husband James. 'He is not allowed to touch it!' she reveals. 'Sometimes I catch him staring at it and I say "No! James!"'

Ola didn't take up dancing until she was twelve, but she remembers that as a child she yearned to try.

'When I was young, I would watch dance programmes and think, "That's what I want to do." So when my school advertised dance classes I really begged my mum to let me go.'

Before taking Chris all the way to the top, Ola danced with DJ Spoony and *GMTV*'s Andrew Castle as well as playing wife swap with Kenny Logan, whose wife Gabby was partnering James.

OLA JORDAN

Six months after her first lesson she had a partner and was already entering youth competitions. At seventeen, she won the Open Polish Championship and was placed twelfth in the World Championships.

Ola split from her dance partner shortly after the World Championships, and was in the process of looking for a new partner when James Jordan phoned her and asked if he could come to Poland. Three weeks later she moved to England.

Ola's parents still live in Poland and rarely come to the UK to watch the show. 'They watch clips of the dance on a Saturday night on the Internet. They don't speak English so they can't understand the judges' comments but they can see how well we danced.'

'Kenny wasn't the best dancer but he was a lovely person,' Ola recalls. 'I enjoyed every minute.'

After a run of married or hooked-up celebs, Ola is hoping for a single dance partner who will make James jealous – and she's aiming high.

'I think Prince Harry would be fabulous. You spend a lot of time with your celebrity, and it is wonderful when you partner someone with a lovely personality. I would also like to have someone who loves dancing just as much as I do. I am quiet and shy offstage, but once I'm on the floor I relax and become extremely open when I dance. Someone who has real confidence will help us on the dance floor and we'll form a great partnership.'

Fiery dancer James is on a mission to match wife Ola's success in series 7, when she partnered champion Chris Hollins.

'I am going to win this year,' he promises. 'I will never live it down if I don't! My wife has won, so now I need to and put my glitterball next to hers.' Despite consistent scores above 30, James and partner Zoe Lucker were the losers in a shock dance off against Ali Bastian in week seven. For James, the *Footballers' Wives* star was 'a dream partner, a hard worker and someone who was not just a dance partner, she became a friend.'

James was born in Gillingham, Kent, and began dancing at age eleven. He and sister Kelly were encouraged by mum Sharon and dad Alan, who had once taught the famous formation team at Peggy

Spencer's dance school. The team were regulars on *Come Dancing* for 40 years but James's parents gave up dancing after having children.

'Kelly started at group dance classes and a friend of mine also attended,' James says. 'I was pushed into going by my parents and at first it was a great laugh, I just went along for the fun and wasn't really that interested.'

Although he began to compete at fourteen, he had little success until he turned eighteen, and began to be motivated by his ability to attract the opposite sex. 'Suddenly I was doing really well in the competitions and I noticed that girls became more interested in me the more successful I became!'

James found a job in the power station where his father worked to fund his classes and recalls, 'The people were fantastic and the job was pure manual labour. I did enjoy it and it was definitely an experience but I wasn't doing it for a career in engineering, I was doing it to pay for my dancing and fund my professional career.'

After turning 21 and moving out of the youth categories, James decided to take a break from competing and stopped dancing with his partner.

'I was fed up with dancing and just wanted a break,' he reveals. 'I had seen Ola dancing and thought she was absolutely amazing. When I split with my partner I immediately thought of Ola.'

After a six-month break he travelled to Poland

to try out with Ola and discovered they were a perfect match. After living in the UK for two years, they turned professional and moved to Hong Kong, to teach.

The prospect of series 8 has brought out his competitive streak in more ways than one. As well as wanting to beat Ola to the trophy, he is itching to take on the new dancers.

'Every year *It Takes Two* asks dancers to compete against each other in challenges. I have won the fitness one and the dance-mat challenge, beating all the boys,' James grins, 'so it's good to be challenged by the new boys.'

A family illness that thwarted plans to leave Australia turned out to be the beginning of Natalie's *Strictly* story. Shortly after shelving the plans to travel to Europe for further dance training, she was chosen as a regular on *Dancing With the Stars,* and she went on to complete seven series before being asked to join the UK *Strictly* family.

'*Dancing With the Stars* changed my life,' she says. 'Over the past few years I have met the most wonderful people. Out of the seven series I have done, I have reached the finals on six occasions and won the show once! The show has opened my eyes and helped me grow for the better. It has taught me a lot and I am very grateful for that.'

Her debut on the UK show was astounding, as she and partner Ricky Whittle bowled the judges over with two spectacular opening performances. Under her tutelage, the *Hollyoaks* star went from strength to strength, narrowly losing out in the final on the public vote.

At six, she found a partner in Jonathan, who went on to appear on *Dancing With the Stars* himself. They bagged many titles and represented Australia for the Taiwan International Championship.

'Jonathon and I had the opening role for a show called the *World's Greatest Dance Spectacular,*' she recalls. 'It was amazing to be so young performing to crowds of six thousand people a night.'

As a junior she danced with a different partner until deciding she would rather dance with brother Glenn. As he was five years older, she immediately joined the adult class. 'Glenn helped me get to a very high standard with his determination and passion for his dancing.'

After coming within a whisker of the glitterball trophy last year, Natalie says, 'I want to have a really great time, put in lots of hard work and try to make it past the finishing line! For me there is nothing more rewarding than seeing the progress in the celebrity – the day they lead you properly – all those little things just make the experience more valuable.'

NATALIE LOWE

Natalie was born in 1980 in Sydney, Australia, into a family of talented dancers. 'I am the youngest child with one older brother Glenn, who I danced with for four years, and sister Kylie, who I used to watch for two years until I was old enough to start,' she says. 'It was only a matter of time before I put on my first pair of dancing shoes. To this day I have never looked back.'

At eight she was representing her country and while her mum and dad had no dance experience themselves, she believes their encouragement was vital. 'They have been nothing but amazing to me with endless support in all aspects of my life and I only have them to thank for this unbelievable journey I am continuing to seek.'

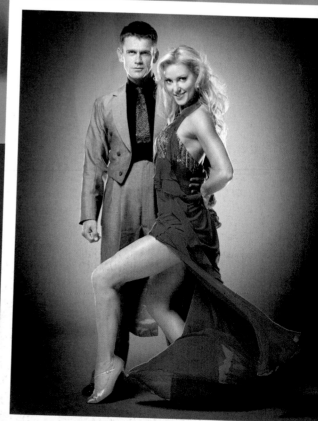

ince winning series 1 with Natasha Kaplinsky, bad boy Brendan has had a mixed bag of celebrity partners ranging from the double-left-footer Fiona Phillips to the stunning and talented Kelly Brook. But he is yet to reclaim the trophy and last year's partner, Jo Wood, was never really a contender. Nonetheless, Brendan clearly adored her, admitting that they had 'a great relationship'.

The hot-blooded hoofer is finally off the market after waltzing Zoe Hobbs down the aisle in June of this year. Jo Wood, Bruce Forsyth, Anton Du Beke and Erin Boag were guests at the wedding ceremony and he even invited long-time adversary Craig Revel Horwood.

'It was a sensational day – quite something,' he recalls. 'We did our first dance to the Michael Buble song "Everything", and it was completely unchoreographed!'

Brendan grew up in Christchurch, New Zealand, in a musical family. Older brother Scott is a dance

BRENDAN COLE

teacher in London and sister Vanessa runs her own dance school. At six, Brendan was dragged kicking and screaming to dance lessons and hated it until he was past his 'gangly, awkward' stage.

He showed a natural talent and started competing at the age of seven. The Cole family soon became famous in the ballroom world and at one point his brother and sister were New Zealand No. 1s, and Brendan was No. 5. At eighteen, Brendan moved to the UK and in 1996 he met Camilla Dallerup. After turning professional, Brendan and Camilla became the New Zealand and Asian Open Professional Champions and were semi-finalists at the International, UK Open, British Open and World Championships.

Ironically, becoming a dancer on *Strictly Come Dancing* has meant more frequent trips home, as he was chosen to be a judge on the New Zealand version of the show.

'It's a great chance to go home and see my family,' he says. 'I also do the odd demonstration spot on the show which is nice.'

Brendan doesn't have many requirements for his ideal celebrity – only that she be 'popular, with stage training, musical, small in stature (for the illegal lifts of course), driven, happy, competitive, elegant, eloquent, lovely, loves the show and doesn't mind being partnered with me (doesn't happen often)… yes I know, it's never going to happen, is it?'

dding even more sparkle to the *Strictly* set this year is DJ and actor Goldie. The larger-than-life star, named after his expensive dental work, has decided to try his hand at ballroom to surprise his fans.

'I love a challenge and I love to do what people don't expect of me,' he explains. 'I think *Strictly* is a total curve ball.'

The 44-year-old has suffered many ups and downs in his varied career, including battling a serious drug

lay in jungle music. The following year he released 'Terminator', which was a huge hit in the jungle scene and featured pioneering use of timestretching, or changing the speed of a note without affecting pitch. Two hit albums followed, *Timeless* and *Saturnz Returns*, and in 1999 he began an acting career with a role as Bond villain Mr Bullion in *The World Is Not Enough*. He then appeared in Guy Ritchie's *Snatch* and in 2001 landed a stint as gangster Angel Hudson in *EastEnders*. More recently he took on the challenge of conducting

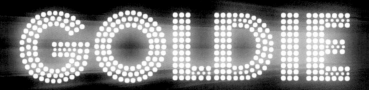

addiction, but now he's back on his feet he's keen to use what he's learnt from his experiences.

'For me personally, coming back into the public eye after rehab it's important to be active,' he says. 'Doing something like this syncs your body and mind. I'm on the way up again and I respect success more. I used to have five cars on my driveway. I'm a lot more down to earth these days.

'The great thing is it's me and I'm always one of those people who like to make people laugh. Also, on a serious note, when I DJ I go out drinking, so this is also going to keep me sober. It's my forty-fifth birthday in September and I feel like I am going to be at my physical peak, which is great.'

Goldie, whose real name is Clifford Price, had a tough upbringing in Walsall, West Midlands. His father left when he was very young and his mum put him up for adoption, so the young Goldie spent many years in care homes. In the early eighties he made a name as a graffiti artist and was featured in the documentary film *Bombing*. Having made his own now-famous set of 'grills' (gold teeth) he went to the States to sell similar moulded molars. In 1991, he moved to London and, after hearing DJ Fabio and Grooverider at the Rage Club, he decided his future

an orchestra in the reality TV show *Maestro*. Joining the series unable to read music and with no knowledge of classical music, he came second but impressed the judges so much he was invited to score a piece for the Proms entitled 'Sine Tempore'.

Goldie has just finished filming the BBC2 series *Goldie's Band – By Royal Appointment* which sees him searching for young people with raw musical talent between the ages of 17 and 24, culminating in a gig at Buckingham Palace in front of Prince Harry.

Despite a background in the music industry, Goldie has not had much dance experience, 'apart from between the ages of eighteen and twenty-two when I was in a professional break-dance crew and it was the first thing I got well known for. The break-dancing gave me great balance and coordination. I throw a few shapes when I go raving, if that counts.'

The DJ is looking forward to letting himself go in the Latin but is not so keen on the idea of ballroom.

'I think I will love the Latin side as I love Latin music,' he says. 'I think ballroom will be tougher but I need to try my best, as things you don't like you have to try hard at. I am in fear of everything ballroom. I watched Peter Schmeichel and I thought "this is really hard". It's too uniform for me.'

But strangely, his biggest worry is about the footwear.

'I am nervous that I have got two left feet,' he admits. 'I am nervous about the first performance and falling over – that would be awful and I would never live it down as after the show I've got to go out and DJ. I have walked in trainers all my life and I hate shoes so wearing them is going to challenge. I want to give one hundred and twenty per cent and I'm worried I will not be able to give one hundred and twenty per cent Goldie.'

But you never know – perhaps Goldie will be able to pull out a 24-carat performance.

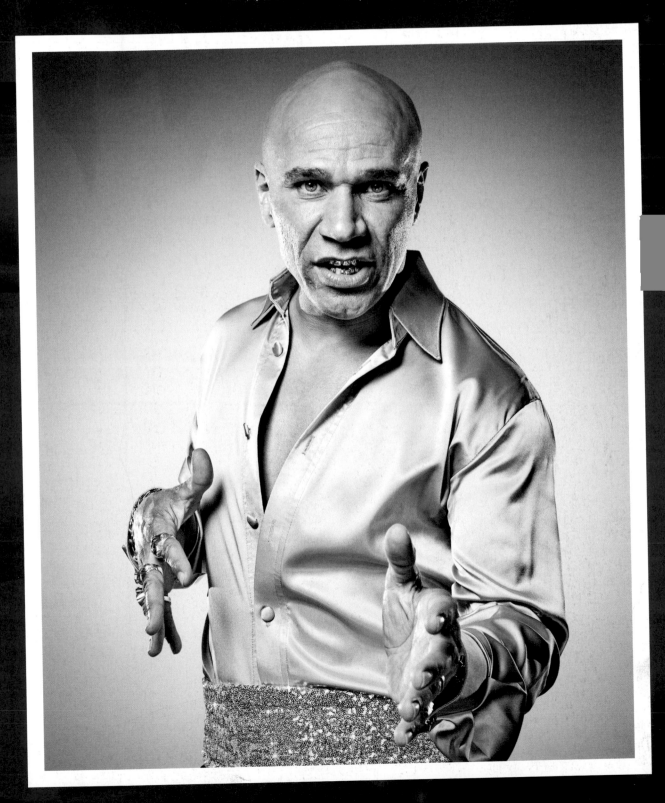

CHRIS HOLLINS

The first thing Chris Hollins did after accepting the challenge of _Strictly Come Dancing_ was abandon his girlfriend Sarah.

'I left her on holiday,' he explains. 'I got a phone call just before we went asking if I would do it, and I said, "Of course." Then they said, "Great. We'll see you on Wednesday!" We were on a dream holiday in Barbados, which we'd booked ages before, and I left her on her own there to go home six days early!'

To add insult to injury, while Chris was waltzing his way through the series, he was also selling his flat, buying another home and moving, with Sarah bearing the brunt of the hard work.

'I managed to complete selling my flat during the first week of _Strictly_ then I got through the first round on Saturday. On Sunday we were putting stuff in storage, then I moved in with my parents and Sarah's brother, so we were shuttling back and forth – and it was like that for eleven weeks before we moved into our house. Sarah had to do it all and she was a legend.'

Viewers of _BBC Breakfast_ news are more used to seeing Chris delivering sports news from the sofa than twirling round the dance floor, but off-screen he has always been a keen sportsman. Years of cricket, football and golf meant his fitness level was fairly high and his attitude to training was spot on, as far as partner Ola Jordan was concerned.

'Ola is a tough teacher but when I first met her I said, "I'm a sportsman. I deal with hard facts, not nicey-nicey. If I'm not doing it right, push me and push me." And she said, "Great. That's what I've been waiting for because I want to win it this year."

'We soon realised that we are soulmates in a way because we like to get the best out of each other. So she was hard on me, but always fair and we really gelled.'

68

A Sporting Dance

But while he was prepared for the arduous training, he admits he was shocked by the all-consuming nature of the show, despite warnings from colleague and previous *SCD* contestant Bill Turnbull. 'Bill told me but I still didn't realise how time-consuming it would be, how mentally exhausting it would be,' Chris says. 'I knew it would be physically tough but I didn't think it would do my head in, trying to remember all the steps, and it really did sometimes.'

Kent-born Chris burst into the series with a passable tango followed by an impressive rumba, which earned him joint top score of 30, along with Ali Bastian. However his 'passionate' expression did attract some comments from the judges, with Craig saying it was 'driving me a bit peculiar' and Bruno telling him he 'looked like he was sucking a lemon'.

After a triumphant opening, however, Chris and Ola nosedived for the next few weeks and it took another seven shows before he bettered his rumba score, with a whopping 34 for his week eight foxtrot in Blackpool. It proved a breakthrough moment for the couple and by the time he reached the quarter-finals Chris was amazed how far he had come.

'Never, ever, ever did I think I would go this far,' he admitted backstage. 'When I first met Ola, I couldn't count to four with the music so I thought we had our work cut out. We always said, "If we can get through the first week, we'll be really happy." Then we got through the first week, then the second and the third and all of a sudden, in the salsa week, I found a bit of confidence and from thereon in we built and built.

'We had a couple of mishaps along the way but then we danced the foxtrot in Blackpool and we thought, "Hey, this is really good."'

Even in their more average weeks, the public got behind the couple, who they dubbed Team Cola, and Ola's *Austin Powers* catchphrase, 'Yeah baby', was soon sweeping the nation.

'Someone posted on the fan website, "Let's support Team Cola", and it got bigger and bigger. Then I got T-shirts made and because everything else was in storage, that's all I had to train in. The catchphrase started because when I danced well Ola said, "Yeah baby!" I didn't realise how big it would be. I'd go to the cinema and as I came out kids ran up to me saying, "Team Cola. Yeah baby!" It was amazing.'

In fact, the audience support meant they were the only couple to avoid the dance off throughout the series.

'It was great that the public were behind us. Everyone told me we had the public support but we honestly never thought about it,' says Chris. 'We never thought about the scores, about where we were, whether we'd get through – it was all about dancing the dance, and making sure we were having really good fun.'

As well as learning the dance routines, Chris had to cope with the ever-decreasing nature of Ola's outfits. The stunning dancer's skimpy catsuits and cut-out dresses are enough to distract any red-blooded male.

69

'The first time I ever saw Ola in one of her outfits was on the photo shoot and she was in a bikini and a bit of ribbon and I thought, "She can't dance like that!"' laughs Chris. 'It did affect my concentration in the rumba, but the funniest one was the red catsuit. I worked really hard at the cha-cha-cha, trying to remember all the steps and I had it really drummed into me. Then I saw her in the dress rehearsal in the red catsuit and I said, "What was the point of my learning all these steps, when everybody is going to be looking at you?" I might just as well have gone on and shuffled about!'

Week eleven saw another breakthrough moment, and one of the most memorable dances ever to grace the *Strictly* dance floor, when Chris tackled the Charleston and earned himself some celebrity fans.

'In training we kept saying "this is our dance",' he recalls. 'It was really what Ola and I are about – having a giggle, enjoying it and putting on a performance – and we had an amazing response. I read in the paper that Vanessa Feltz cried with joy!

'I went in to *BBC Breakfast* the following Monday and Spandau Ballet, one of my favourite groups when I was a lad, were there. They all said, "Mate, your Charleston was brilliant!" That was so weird.'

Despite the celebrated dance, the magic 10 eluded the couple until the final, when they came head to head with Ricky Whittle and Natalie Lowe.

'I did think that we'd never get a ten because I know I'm not very good. I remember talking to Natalie when they'd had a bad round in the rock 'n' roll – they were still excellent but by their standards it was ordinary. They'd got a seven and Natalie said "That's my first ever seven." That was week eleven. By then, Ola and I were still *pleased* if we got a seven!

'Ola missed the first ten because we were thinking about taking on Ricky Whittle in the final. I kept saying, "I just don't want to be humiliated." She told me, "Just

do your best." Then Ricky went out for the first dance, his quickstep, which I still think is the best dance I have ever seen on *Strictly*, and it got five tens. I was thinking, "Oh my God. How do we follow that?" So when the first ten came along, we were too focused on what we were doing next to realise.'

A triumphant Charleston bagged them the perfect score of 50, and after a thrilling final, with four dances each, the public vote made Chris and Ola the 2010 *Strictly Come Dancing* champs.

'You know when people say, "It was all a bit of a blur"? Now I know what they mean,' says an incredulous Chris. 'The whole week was a blur of filming and training – four dances, oh my God!

'Until Thursday night I still didn't have my show dance finished. And then all of a sudden we were standing there, on Saturday night, with all the dances over, and I could relax. Then I heard "Chris and Ola" and, as you probably saw on our faces, both of us were in complete shock. Ola grabbed me and started crying, there was all this confetti coming down and suddenly they present you with the trophy – it was absolutely amazing.'

For 'Mrs Jordan' or 'Olachops', as Chris affectionately called his partner, it was a highly emotional moment.

'My black shirt had to be wrung out because it was full of Ola's tears,' jokes Chris. 'It's very difficult to relate to anybody who hasn't done it, how much effort the professionals put into their partners. They not only have to get the music right, they have to get the choreography right and then they have

to teach their partner. By the end, they are tired, emotional, and they desperately want to win. I know how much it meant to Ola. She's always wanted to win it – she told me that every day. At the final she said, "You've made my dream come true, you've done it for me." Even I had to hold back the tears then.

'Ola is a beautiful, beautiful woman and she has a heart to match. She is fantastic.'

THE JUDGES' VERDICT

LEN ON WEEK ONE RUMBA

'You were like two lovely dancing Hobbits – I loved it.'

CRAIG ON CHRIS'S TANGO

'The facial expressions were driving me a bit peculiar. It was very trout mouth all the way through.'

ALESHA ON THE CHARLESTON

'I've seen a whole new side to you. You owned that dance. For the first Charleston, you've set the standard.'

DARCEY ON THE FINAL CHARLESTON

'You transported me to the golden era of the movies. That dance was made for you.'

BRUNO ON THE FINAL FOXTROT

'I want to take this moment to congratulate Ola – you've turned a frog into a prince. Elegant, charming and beautifully danced.'

t's the battle of the soap sirens as *Corrie* cutie Tina O'Brien goes up against *EastEnders* vamp Kara Tointon. But Tina is not yet eyeing up the opposition.

'It is such a big task and at the moment I'm just looking to get through the first week,' she explains.

'I've never been in a competition so I have no idea how competitive I'm going to get. Of course I want to win, but I just want to concentrate on learning the dance moves. At the moment all I want to do

Having enjoyed dance as a child, she can't wait to learn new styles – and try on all the posh frocks.

'The reason that I am taking part in *Strictly* is that it is something completely different. I have always wanted to learn to dance properly but just never had the opportunity.

'It's going to take me completely out of my comfort zone. As a child I was absolutely crazy about dancing. I used to visit my gran who lived in sheltered accommodation and I'd take my CD player and dance for her. I

is do well for myself. And I am also looking forward to getting in shape.'

As well as being young, pretty and reasonably fit, Tina is the only one of the contestants who boasts a GCSE in dance!

'I did a dance GCSE at school but it was more expressionist dance, like trees blowing in the wind,' she laughs. 'I think I am quite a good mover when I have had a drink and definitely like to have a dance when I am out.'

The 27-year-old actress was born and raised in Manchester and began acting as a teenager with a role in children's hospital drama *The Ward*. In 1999, at the age of sixteen, she joined the cast of *Coronation Street* as sixteen-year-old schoolgirl Sarah-Louise Platt, the daughter of Gail. During her time on the cobbles, Tina's character had a baby at thirteen, was the victim of Internet grooming, lost a second baby after finding out her fiancé was gay and came close to death, along with her whole family, at the hands of murderous maniac Richard Hillman, played by ex-*Strictly* celeb Brian Capron.

Tina left the soap in 2007 and had a baby daughter, Scarlett, with co-star Ryan Thomas in 2008. She is now starring in *Waterloo Road*.

had absolutely no fear and I really would love to have that freedom again.

'I am also of course really excited by the prospect of wearing all the costumes as I have always loved dressing up!'

While her most famous character was more of a girl next door than a femme fatale, Tina has twice ranked in *FHM*'s Top 100 Sexiest Women in the World and is looking to bring some red-hot Latin action to the floor.

'I think I will definitely like Latin more because it's more fun and flirty and sexy whereas ballroom is more regimented and looks quite stiff. Latin looks more fiery and from the soul.'

As an actress, her biggest worry is having to be herself on-screen.

'This is so new to me and I am not sure what to expect,' she admits. 'I'm worried that I am not going to be able to hide behind a character, which makes me feel vulnerable as the judges are going to be commenting on me, not the character I'm playing, but I can only do my best. I just hope my nerves won't stop my personality coming through.'

With millions of *Corrie* fans wishing her well, Tina is sure to be a favourite.

SPORT RELIEF
does STRICTLY COME DANCING

The glitterball trophy got a makeover in March when it became a sparkling red nose for a very special edition of *Strictly*. In the name of charity, rival Dragons Peter Jones and Duncan Bannatyne swapped the boardroom for the ballroom, to come head to head in Sport Relief does *Strictly Come Dancing*. And the fire-breathing entrepreneurs began the challenge with a lot of hot air.

Peter, who was paired with finalist Natalie Lowe, revealed, 'My relationship with Duncan has always been like a relationship you'd have with an ex-wife – you know you have to get on, but you don't particularly like each other.'

Lilia Kopylova's partner Duncan boasted, 'I'm a better businessman than him, better looking than him and more successful than him – and now he's going to learn I'm also a better dancer than him!'

In training for the tango, however, Peter managed to put his back out and Natalie began to panic about the lack of time left to learn the routine. But the *Dragons' Den* star wasn't going to go down without a fight. 'To be honest, coming into it I didn't think there was much competition until, of course, I put my back out,' he said before the dance off. 'I went straight to the physio but even if they have to carry me off on a stretcher, Duncan isn't going to win!'

On the night, Tess pointed out another disadvantage the telecommunications mogul has: his height.

'Peter Jones has got youth on his side but he is also six foot seven and has size fourteen feet,' she revealed. 'Good luck, Natalie.'

Despite his back injury, Peter kicked off proceedings with a tantalising tango to the strains of

the classic Beatles track, 'Money (That's What I Want)'.

Head judge Len Goodman was reasonably impressed and told him, 'For a very tall man you did a very good job.'

Bruno and Craig, however, had more searing remarks. 'That tango was even less convincing than Jordan's wedding,' joked Bruno. 'What's wrong with your legs? It looks like you were dying for a pee!'

Craig added, 'All the Ls, starting with lanky. It was laboured, it was lame, it was lacklustre, but two things were good. The left was very good and your timing was great, so well done.' After a mediocre score of 16 was announced, Peter remarked, 'I'm happy – as long as Duncan gets 15!'

Duncan and Lilia chose the cha-cha-cha for their dance and they soon discovered that the notoriously dour Scotsman had teeth. But his newfound smile had an odd effect on his dance partner. 'My cha-cha has some really sexy moves. Not many people start dancing when they're sixty,' he said. 'The only problem is every time I smile Lilia starts laughing.'

In fact, his cheeky cha-cha-cha raised many a smile and a good few laughs along the way and, with the tables turned on him by the judges, the grouchy Dragon was in for a slaying.

Len could hardly contain his amusement as he told Duncan, 'Dragons' Den and Strictly are a bit similar. You come out, you show us your product, you make your pitch and then you decide whether you want to invest the same as us. I can't invest too much in that cha-cha, I'm sorry.'

Bruno commented, 'It was like Quasimodo trying to keep up with Esmerelda. It will go down in history as one of the worst cha-cha-chas ever – but I quite liked it.'

And Craig joked, 'That grinding at the beginning was grotesque, darling. There need to be more basic

steps in the routine, the step-touches were abysmal, there was no real connection between you, it was completely devoid of any hip action, the free arm was a mess, as was the timing, but apart from all of those things, it was perfect!'

With a meagre score of 10 out of 30, the older Dragon was finally slayed by the public vote, a fate he took in good humour. All in all the evening raised over £31 million for good causes and also allowed Natalie Lowe, who had narrowly missed out on a win in the series 7 final, to get her hands on the trophy at last.

'It was a great challenge which meant a lot to me, as it was for a great cause,' she said.

Kristina was born in Siberia and studied ballet before moving on to Latin and standard styles, as well as Rhythm and Theatre Arts. At seven, she began to compete and was soon renowned in the far eastern Russian province. By sixteen, she was teaching dance but she always studied hard for a back-up career, earning a Masters degree in Tourism and Hospitality.

In her twenties she was invited to compete in the US and moved to Seattle. In 2004, she and her partner represented the US in 'the most prestigious competition in the professional dance world', the World Exhibition at the Blackpool Dance Festival in the Theatre Style category. She then returned to international-style Latin with a new partner, Michael Wentink, one of Latin dance's most famous masters, and together they won the South African Championship and reached the semi-finals at the 2007 British Open in Blackpool.

The stunning Siberian joined *Strictly* in 2008, and got a rude awakening when she was partnered with people's hero John Sergeant. The

KRISTINA RIHANOFF

Last year's partnership with boxer Joe Calzaghe proved a knockout, as the pair fell in love. The 'champ and the vamp' left in week 5, but Kristina has no complaints about her beefy celebrity partner. 'I feel like a winner,' she smiles. 'I'm in a beautiful relationship.'

Since the end of the last series, the Russian minx has been helping Joe with his charity work for a local children's hospital near his home in Wales, as well as taking part in the *Strictly* tour, dancing with former winner Mark Ramprakash. She followed that with the Pro Tour, where she had a fabulous time.

'I'm so proud of the Pro Tour, she says. 'It was such hard work but a fantastic experience.'

political broadcaster managed to avoid getting chucked off before voluntarily quitting in week 9. Her debut series was an education for the talented teacher.

'I learnt *Strictly Come Dancing* is not only about dancing but also popularity,' she explains. 'John knew how to connect with the public. He was kind and respectful, you can't wish for anything better. He was my ideal partner for my first series.'

This year Kristina is hoping it will be third time lucky and she plans to go all the way. 'I have lots of desire and energy to take someone all the way to the final this year.'

With a penchant for revealing Latin outfits, new dancer Robin is hoping to get hot, hot, hot on the dance floor. And he has a worrying warning for self-confessed 'fuddy-duddy' Len Goodman.

'I think I could be one of the more controversial dancers on the show,' Robin promises. 'I'm looking forward to shaking things up and bringing some hot and sexy moves to the dance floor, but I'm sure my mum won't be too happy with me getting my body out on display!'

Although he prefers to see himself as a Latin lover, he struggled to lose the tag of the perfect ballroom dancer as a lad.

'I didn't look like this when I was younger – I was really slim with lots of hair,' he explains. 'I looked like a proper ballroom boy.'

Even so, he still loves some of the traditional ballroom dances, as they bring out the romantic in him. 'Some people say the rumba is the dance of

ROBIN WINDSOR

love. But for me the waltz is the real dance of love. I'm a romantic at heart and love telling a good love story.'

Born and raised just outside Ipswich, Robin attended the local dance school from the age of three before moving to the Ipswich School of Dance. At fifteen he moved to London and had a successful youth career for five years before retiring from competitive dancing. At 22, Robin won a role in a major touring dance show which travelled the world.

'Walking out on to a Broadway stage for the first time was one of the most amazing experiences of my life,' he recalls. It also led him to perform on the Australian *Dancing With the Stars*, as well as *So You Think You Can Dance* in Holland.

When it comes to choosing an ideal celebrity there's one girl he can't get out of his head.

'Kylie would be my ideal dance partner,' he says. 'Failing that I'll settle for someone who just has a bit of rhythm! A musician or a pop star would make the perfect celebrity dance partner because of their natural understanding of music.'

The 30-year-old newcomer has met his professional co-stars already and is looking forward to working with them. 'I was feeling really nervous before I met all the other professionals,' he admits. 'But they have all been so welcoming to me and I can't wait to start dancing with my new pro partner, Kristina.'

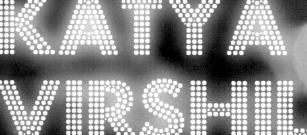

Lithuanian-born Katya made her *Strictly Come Dancing* debut last year with a larger-than-life celebrity partner. Paired with cricketer Phil Tufnell, they managed to get through to week 9 despite a serious knee injury which required an operation.

'I had such an amazing time dancing with Tuffers but this year I want to go even further,' she vows. 'My ideal celebrity would be another big personality!'

Born in Lithuania in 1983, Katya's family moved to Israel when she was six and she began classes in jazz, ballet and modern dance. Seven years later they moved to Vancouver in Canada, and Katya went to see her first Latin American competition.

'I remember watching Tony Meredith and Melanie LaPatin [four-time North American Latin Champions] in a competition,' she recalls. 'Melanie was wearing this beautiful sequin gown – and the glamour took my breath away. My mother took me to my first class, and I was wildly intimidated because everyone was so good. On top of that, since I was about three

In 2003, Katya moved into movies, training Richard Gere and Jennifer Lopez for *Shall We Dance*, as well as appearing on screen. She went on to choreograph and train the cast for the acclaimed

years older than the other kids, the instructor told me I was too old and would never accomplish anything.'

Despite this, within three years she was the youngest-ever British Columbian Latin Dance Champion and at 17 she won the Canadian Latin Championship, earning herself a place at the World Championships representing Canada in St Petersburg, Russia.

While competing in Russia she developed a passion for teaching youngsters which later led to her forming her own dance school.

'Teaching children and teens to dance is a necessity in my life,' she insists. 'The children relate to me and I can show them the cool side of dancing.'

drama *Take the Lead*, performing an unforgettable tango with Antonio Banderas in the movie.

After being spotted by top Bollywood choreographer, Shiamak Davar, she was invited to set up Latin dance workshops across India as well as performing in his stage production, *I Believe*, which drew more than 60,000 spectators.

Partnered with Brendan Cole for the professional dances in the last series, Katya is switching partners for season 8 and breaking in new boy Artem Chigvintsev. 'I'm so excited to have Artem as my professional dancing partner this year,' she says. 'Although I'm sure Brendan will be a bit jealous!'

He may be one of the new kids on the block but being paired with Artem Chigvintsev won't be an easy ride. 'All I want is someone who can work hard,' he warns. 'I'm a workaholic and will stay in the training room all night long if I have to! All celebrities bring different strengths. Sport people can be rehearsed twenty-four seven, a singer will know how to move and an actress will have all the performance skills. The most important thing is to find out what they're good at, find their individual talents and make the most of them.'

Latin specialist Artem grew up in Russia and was encouraged to dance by his mother, who wanted him to have a hobby to keep him on the straight and narrow. He found he loved the dance classes and, when he began to win competitions, he decided to take it up as a career. At 15 he travelled the world, training for his future. 'Dancing has taken me all over... I have trained in England, Italy, Germany and many other countries.'

ARTEM CHIGVINTSEV

In 2004 he moved to Los Angeles where he trained and taught dance before becoming a finalist on the first series of *So You Think You Can Dance*, and he has since worked as a choreographer on the show. '*So You Think You Can Dance* was such an amazing opportunity for me,' he recalls. 'It taught me so much about the world of professional dancing in Hollywood.' Working in LA also brought some acting roles, including one where he was seduced by the cougars of Orange County in *The OC*. More recently he has performed in a dance show on a worldwide tour, performing on Broadway and the West End stage.

The 28-year-old dancer is thrilled to be joining the *Strictly* family for the first time.

'Being asked to take part in *Strictly* came as a massive surprise,' he admits. 'I can't wait to start training.'

His favourite Latin is the paso doble because it is 'full of character – it's so theatrical and dramatic'. In ballroom he enjoys the tango and the foxtrot as 'the tango totally characterises elegance whereas the foxtrot is more chilled and graceful'.

Away from the dance floor he enjoys all things car-related, especially Formula One racing. And his ideal celebrity is a pop singer and F1 wag.

'Nicole Scherzinger would be my ideal dance partner – but as she has just won *Dancing With the Stars* it would probably be a bit unfair on the others!'

avin Henson follows a long line of rugby players who have taken to the dance floor, and he has a lot to live up to. Austin Healey just missed out on the quarter-finals in series 6 and Matt Dawson made it all the way to the final, losing out to Mark Ramprakash.

'I am feeling a bit under pressure because all of the other rugby players that have taken part in *Strictly* have done really well,' he admits. 'But I have no idea how I will do.

'I have no dance experience at all and no idea if I can do this. I'm up for the challenge and I just hope I can pick it up.

'I love listening to music, especially listening to the lyrics, but with dancing it's all about listening to the beat.'

While some beefier celebs balk at the spray tan, Gavin will have no such reservations. He likes the fake bake so much he even took some to Norway, where he braved snow and ice for the reality show *71 Degrees North*.

'Spray tan? I love it!' he admits. 'It was considered strange in rugby circles when I was about eighteen, but now everyone grooms themselves. I get stick, yeah, but everyone does it!'

Gavin's experience in the sub-zero reality show was the reason he decided to take on the *Strictly* challenge.

'In the show ten celebs went to Norway and tried to survive in freezing conditions,' he explains. 'I loved the whole experience; I got lots out of it and got on really well with the group of people taking part – I hope that this experience will be the same. Also, I thought it would be really good to learn how to dance and then go bust some moves on the

dance floor without first having to lose my inhibitions through drink!'

The Welsh International began playing rugby at school in Bridgend and at eighteen was sought out by three professional clubs, Maesteg, Llanelli and Swansea. He chose Swansea RFC, even though they were offering the least pay. In 2001, he made his debut for Wales and, at the end of the season, was named the International Board's Young Player of the Year. Gavin switched to the Ospreys when regional rugby was launched in Wales and in 2005 he helped his country win the coveted Six Nations cup.

But his career on the pitch has been plagued by injury and his 2005 British Lions tour of New Zealand was cut short by a groin strain. A year later, an Achilles tendon injury interrupted his season and in 2007 he was deemed unfit for the World Cup squad. Another injury meant that Gavin missed the Wales tour of South Africa in the summer of 2008. He played just three tests in the 2009 Six Nations and was ruled out of the British & Irish Lions tour of South Africa with an ankle injury.

While injuries were filling the back pages of the papers, his private life was providing a few front-page headlines as his five-year relationship with singer Charlotte Church came to an end in March 2010. The couple have two children together – Ruby, three, and Dexter, born January 2009.

Frustrated by his recurring problems, Gavin has taken eighteen months off from the game, and his weight has dropped by three stone, so he is one contestant who is not keen to trim any pounds during training.

'I am only used to doing an hour of training each day,' he says. 'I might struggle with the long hours.

I'm conscious that people lose weight doing this show but I don't want to lose any weight.'

The 28-year-old is looking forward to the energetic dances but thinks he might struggle with the more romantic holds.

'I would love to be able to be a Latin dancer. But realistically I think I will be better at ballroom as I will be in the "hold" and my partner can keep me in check. The close, more intimate dances might be a bit strange. That sort of physical contact is definitely something I will have to try and come to terms with.'

Dance partner Katya will certainly be happy to show him how!

bombastic bruno

'We are going to get plenty of excitement, drama, surprises and great dancing,' declared Bruno Tonioli as the first show of series 7 opened. As usual the effusive Italian provided a few memorable moments himself.

Leaping out of his seat on numerous occasions, Bruno shocked new judge Alesha in the first show when he grabbed her arm to demonstrate a waltz hold to Martina Hingis. And he hid his face in embarrassment after telling Phil Tufnell, 'You're great to look at.' He reduced Lynda Bellingham to tears with his 'Carry on matron' comment and fell out with Craig and Len numerous times.

Even flying frequently back and forth from the States, where Bruno was also judging *Dancing With the Stars*, couldn't dampen the spirits of the excitable Italian. He was impressed by the standard of many of the celebrity dancers, and thought sports presenter Chris Hollins was a deserved winner of the glitterball.

'Chris came out very strong in the end,' he said. 'I think his entertainment value, more than dance technique, captured the imaginations of the judges and the public and that's what the show is about – somebody that comes from nowhere, and ends up being extremely entertaining! He had a great attitude. It was a close call but I think his charm won it.'

ON CHRIS HOLLINS' LINDY HOP
'Chris, you really crack me up. It was like watching a cheeky frantic monkey. But I loved it – it was like a scene out of The Jungle Book. I wanted to throw you a banana.

AFTER PHIL TUFNELL'S SAMBA
'It's not Daddy Cool, it's daddy well-oiled. Anything goes.'

AFTER JOE CALZAGHE'S TANGO
'The champ and the vamp – potential for steam and I'm getting damp. The most boring tango I've ever seen.'

AFTER LAILA ROUASS' CHA-CHA-CHA
'I cannot believe the waste of all that magnificent equipment! It's like having a Ferrari and driving at twenty miles an hour.'

bruno's thoughts on series 7

Who was the best dancer?

Ricky the *Hollyoaks* hunk. Ricky Whittle was amazing, he was a great all-rounder, he got the girls going, he had a fiery personality and was very competitive. Then again, Chris Hollins was the man of the people and the one who had the most support. Fans get very into the journey, the unexpected. Ricky had it all, the look of a champ, but Chris came from nowhere and it was incredibly surprising and very, very entertaining! In this show, of course, it's about the competition but also you can catch people's imagination in many different ways, and with this you need a great performance, then you improve and improve.

Who was the biggest surprise?

Jade Johnson having to retire was a shock. She had a talent and I thought she had a good chance. She was doing very, very well and it was sad that she didn't have the opportunity to continue and improve on her talent. She really had everything going for her. It was a bit of a disappointment but these things happen. It was a terrible shame because we all thought she would make the final.

AFTER RICKY WHITTLE'S SALSA

'It's not Ricky Whittle it's Ricky Martin. Hips like lethal weapons.'

AFTER JADE JOHNSON'S SAMBA

'Talk about the woman on top – you were driving it. She's on it. You were showing beautiful things. Plenty. Hot.'

Who was the worst dancer?

We had a pretty good line-up for the worst dancer this year! Maybe we should do a special and show them all. Jo Wood should go in the Hall of Fame with the best of the worst. Poor Jo had no sense of rhythm and no musicality. Nice lady, but a complete dance disaster!

Biggest trier?

Craig Kelly kept going and going but it never clicked in, he never really got into gear. At least he got to Blackpool, so he danced in his home town. He had plenty of determination but there was a disconnection between his head and his legs.

How did Alesha do as judge?

I think she did very, very well and did a very good job. The first time round can be tricky, because we've all been doing it for years and she came out and she held her own and that's what you have to do.

How was Darcey's judging?

It was lovely to have Darcey because she is a wonderful dancer but I think four judges is enough. Having too many dilutes it all too much and you have nothing to say because it's all been covered! There is only so much you can say about one dance.

BEHIND THE SCENES
The Rehearsals

The view from the leather sofa, on the other side of the camera in the red room

As Jade was forced to retire from the competition in week nine, Ian sits back and watches the other couples nervously rehearse

White markers show Jess, the celeb and their partner where to stand to be in camera shot.

'This week we were the most advanced we've been in the whole twelve weeks,' he says. 'We had our two routines done by Monday and normally we're still cleaning it up on Wednesday. I have to work on Sundays because I'm filming *Hollyoaks* twelve hours a day – so I'm knackered already. We can only train for a limited time in the evening so while everyone else can train from ten to six I only get three hours.'

Laila and Anton practise their American smooth as Chris chats to a camera man

In the early part of the afternoon, just hours before the nerve-racking quarter-finals begin, the couples take every opportunity they can to practise their moves on the studio dance floor. Dressed in a vest top and jeans, Ricky is busy perfecting his cha-cha-cha with Natalie. Outside in the corridor, Laila and Anton are preparing for their American smooth.

While he will never miss an opportunity for a run-through, *Hollyoaks* hunk Ricky reckons they cracked the routines relatively early this week, despite a hectic filming schedule on his day job.

As the professional dancers rehearse the group waltz, the girls test out their dresses so any adjustments can be made before the live show

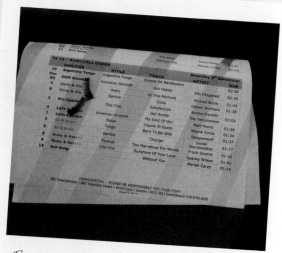

The music programme for the live quarter-final – timing is vital

On the sidelines, Brian watches them go through their paces as the band practises 'Get Happy' in preparation for the show. His partner Ali is still in hair and make-up, but the American dancer reveals that, after a difficult week dealing with her injured foot, they have finally nailed it.

'We've had a lot of stress this week,' he says. 'It's been a tough week with two dances to learn. Ali still has the bruising on her foot so it's been frustrating, stopping and starting. But yesterday after camera rehearsal we had a little sneak run-through, we trained for another couple of hours and suddenly everything came together beautifully.

The view from the orchestra before the audience arrives

The rehearsal is also the time the live orchestra can practise their crucial part in the show

Lights, camera, action! A cameraman prepares for the live run-through

Brian and Ali relax after a smooth rehearsal

Back in his dressing room the reality of the quarter-finals has hit Chris. And musing about the final is strictly against the rules of Mrs Jordan.

'I'm not allowed to say the "f-word" around Ola,' laughs Chris. 'We're taking it week by week and this is going to be a really tough one. Two dances, and there are no mugs out there any more. I think I'm the only mug there! We're like a herd of antelopes and the lions have been picking off the weak ones – I am the baby one with the limp. I just know that eventually we are going to get chewed up.'

Sizing up the competition, he ponders, 'Ricky and Ali are premier league and I think they've been awesome. Laila is a beautiful ballroom dancer but she has struggled with Latin, and I have had my own struggles so it's tough. We have a Latin and a ballroom this week and you can't afford any bad dances.

'I can't believe I'm having this conversation, sitting talking about being in the last four. It's crazy.'

As the 2 p.m. dress run approaches, the dancers are all in full costume and Ricky and Chris are scraping the bottoms of their dancing shoes with a wire brush, to give them a better grip on the floor.

The stalls, which will soon be filled with 550 eager fans, are empty except for one or two of those working on the show. As the judges are not allowed to see the dances before the live performance, the judges' table, replaced with a larger one this year to fit in fifth judge Darcey Bussell, is manned by members of the crew.

After a stunning opening cha-cha-cha from five of the professional couples, Bruce takes over

'That happens most weeks – either that or it falls apart, one of the two!'

By now it's no secret that Ali and Brian have become incredibly close, and he admits he couldn't wish for a better partner.

'Ali is fantastic, but she's got a tremendous amount of natural talent anyway,' he says. 'I couldn't be happier. When you get someone who is young, beautiful and talented it is an absolute bonus but the

Ricky waits nervously on the other side of the grand stair case

Chris scuffs the bottoms of his shoes with a wire brush to give him better grip and passes the time watching the snooker.

real bonus is when you get someone that you love spending time with and you get along with perfectly.

'When you go in to train for eight hours a day with the same person, it's important that you get along. If you have chemistry, then that makes things easier.'

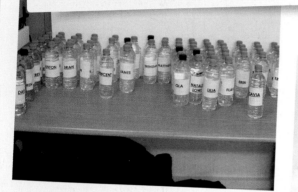

Crew members stand in for the five judges during the run-through

Each celeb and dancer has a stash of water bottles backstage to keep them hydrated

proceedings and introduces the remaining four couples. For the purposes of timing he begins to tell a joke about Ali and Brian but stops short of the punchline, explaining he wants to get a proper reaction from the couple on the night.

With over 60 years of dancing behind him, Bruce knows his steps and he gives encouragement and tips to all the celebrities. 'Keep the aggressive face,' he advises Ali before she kicks off the rehearsal with the tango. 'Bad rehearsal, good show,' he tells Laila after she messes up some steps in the salsa. 'I've depended on that all my life.'

Chris thrusts his pelvis at the imaginary audience during the samba and Bruce jokes, 'Whoever is in chair thirteen is going to get it!'

From the sidelines, Laura Solari, Lisa Armstrong and Nadia Nigoumi are watching closely. The dress run is an invaluable way of spotting glitches in the hair, make-up and costume before the live show – and there are plenty of niggles to worry about.

One of Ali's hair extensions threatens to fall off during her samba; Natalie Lowe's hair has begun to come down before her performances and, during the foxtrot, her heel gets caught in her hem with disastrous results for the dance.

'That didn't go as well as it should have done,' says Ricky after the run-through. 'Apart from that, it is a beautiful routine and it will be lovely when we do it properly.'

Wardrobe have their work cut out, literally, as they fix the various snags that have cropped up. First job is to remove a swathe of material from the bottom of Natalie's dress to prevent the heel catching again. Ola, who is used to wearing skimpy outfits, wanders in complaining her ballroom gown for the waltz is too heavy, and the girls cut three layers from the full skirt. Finally they manage to knock up a perfect pair of gloves for Laila.

Hair, of course, has to be fixed before the dancers go onstage for the live show. 'It wasn't the best dress rehearsal,' says Laura. 'I tidied Natalie's hair and re-tonged the fringe; I took Ali's out entirely and reset the whole head. Flavia's needed rejigging but it has just about the right amount of curl now.

'It's good that we can work with the celebrities and dancers over and over, because I come to understand how their hair behaves. For example, I know Kristina would need a complete reset because her hair just won't hold curl. We have redone pretty much everyone but that's okay because we expect it. It's normal and sometimes it's good that the dress run goes badly because you know that you can fix everything for the show.

'I'd hate it if it all went perfectly because we wouldn't learn anything and if it goes wrong we wouldn't have expected it and put a plan into place. So it's much better if the dress run goes badly!'

Anton watches television with some of the crew as he waits for his turn to rehearse

tunning Kara Tointon was named Sexiest Soap Actress in 2008 so she is bound to set a few pulses racing as she takes to the dance floor. And she has already had a taste of *Strictly* glory, having won the Sport Relief version in 2008, partnering former champ Mark Ramprakash. But it also gave her an insight into the struggle ahead.

'When I did Sport Relief with Mark Ramprakash I did Latin and that was so hard,' she recalls. 'Karen

'I have been a huge fan of the show for years,' she says. 'In fact, when I joined *EastEnders* I had a friend in it every year and I used to live for it every Saturday. I just adore the show and have always been a massive fan and always dreamed that I would get the opportunity one day.

'I used to watch my mum and dad do the jive, and I always thought it was really cool and I wish that nowadays we could have a dance that the guys and girls could go out and do at a nightclub. This

Hardy was teaching us and she is so good at it and I wasn't comfortable, but I think you have to let go in the Latin. I have really got a lot to learn because I just want to enjoy it.

'With ballroom, I have never done any of it, so I am intrigued to see if I am any good. But I love how graceful and beautiful it is so I am really looking forward to it.

'The one that scares me is the jive as it's really fast and jumpy. I am just not looking forward to that at all but looking forward to conquering it if I can.'

Kara was born in Basildon, Essex and started speech and drama lessons at the age of seven. Her first professional job was dancing in *Snow White* at the age of eleven and in the same year she made a brief appearance in *EastEnders* as a school friend of Sonia, played by former *Strictly* contestant Natalie Cassidy. Ten years later, in 2004, Kara returned to the Square as sexy 'tart with a heart' Dawn Swann. After conning the locals into paying for her boob job, being kidnapped by a lover who planned to give her an enforced Caesarean and various affairs with male residents, Dawn 'swanned' off into the sunset in 2009.

Having watched many of her co-stars on previous shows, Kara is thrilled that her turn has come.

show is bringing that back as there is something lovely about getting up on a dance floor at a wedding and being able to jive, or do something really special.'

Although she did a little dancing as a child, most of Kara's current experience is a Saturday night boogie in a club.

'I did the normal tap, ballet and modern dancing when I was growing up, and stopped that at sixteen when I left school,' she reveals. 'I always wanted to learn the ballroom side of things, but it's so specialised and people go into that kind of thing at an early age.

'I have got this place I always go to called Little Italy in Soho. It's the only place I go and about once a month we go down there and dance all night – I love it.

'Whether I am any good, I have no idea but I just know I love dancing, and when music is on I just jig to it. Any Beyoncé song would get me moving.'

The tough training is one hurdle but, for the nervous actress, the worst part will be the judges' comments – even if they are good!

'I am not competitive but am competitive with myself,' she says. 'I am not good with criticism but over the years with acting you get so much rejection and get told to change this and adapt that, so slowly I have started to appreciate criticism and think,

"Okay, they are just trying to make you better."
'With the judges I don't know how I am going to cope so it's going to be interesting. I think it will be embarrassing if they give you a nice comment, and also embarrassing if they give you an awful one so I can't really win. I guess you just

need to soak it up. For me it's about getting as far as I can, learning as many dances as I can and to have a skill that I have never had before. I am looking forward to being at a party and whipping out my new moves.'

Flame-haired beauty Aliona Vilani, who certainly stands out on the dance floor, is looking forward to her second season of *Strictly Come Dancing*. 'I had the best time of my life,' she says. 'I don't know how this year can possibly be any better!'

The Russian doll was partnered with Rav Wilding for her debut season and thinks that the judges may have been shocked by her risqué style of choreography. In fact, Craig mentioned the 'filth-ridden gyrations' in their rumba and Len told her off for adding an illegal lift in their first dance, the tango, but she believes they will know what to expect this time around.

Sadly, the bulky *Crimewatch* presenter was not the best dancer and, having survived their first dance off, the couple were eliminated in the third week.

'Rav was such a lovely guy,' says Aliona. 'It was such a shame to go out so early.'

Aliona was born in May 1984 in Russia and at the age of five was enrolled in an 'arts gymnasium' for classical ballet and performing arts. Six years later she

In the Latin, she loves the cha-cha-cha because it 'has a lot of different sides to it' but her favourite dance is the waltz.

'Each dance has this certain something special,' she explains. 'It's almost like having secrets for yourself in each dance that you let the people in on for a moment when you're performing. I would have to say my favourite is the waltz, because it just takes you into this special dreamy wonderland where you can get away from your everyday life. The cha-cha-cha in itself is a very cheeky and flirtatious dance and also can have the party feel of samba, the elegance of rumba, the arrogance of the paso doble and rock 'n' roll feel of jive.'

The 26-year-old dancer says she would like her partner in the forthcoming series of *Strictly* 'to be able to follow my innovative ideas – and keep up with me' and to be 'physically prepared to take challenges and break limits'.

ALIONA VILANI

took up ballroom and was soon competing in junior competitions in Eastern Europe. At thirteen, she was invited to join the Kaiser Dance Academy in New York and moved to the States. She then studied salsa, hip-hop and jazz at the Broadway Dance Center and became US Junior Ten-Dance Champion shortly afterwards.

In 2001 she was chosen by the National Dance Congress to be a member of the ballroom team, which went on to win a world amateur championship title, and soon afterwards she turned professional. In 2006, she moved to Los Angeles to continue competing and teaching. Before joining *Strictly* she performed professional routines on *Dancing With the Stars* in the States.

'Jonny Wilkinson would be a great partner because he is a very dedicated sportsman,' she says. 'Andy Murray would also be great.'

American swing champ Jared Murillo comes from a very different background to most of the *Strictly* stable, having already performed in smash hit movies *High School Musical* and *High School Musical 2*. He also took to the stage for the *HSM* tour and was an all-singing, all-dancing member of Vocal Adrenaline in the US tour of *Glee*.

His previous experience of teaching includes choreographing co-star Zac Efron and until recently he was dating Ashley Tisdale, who plays the fabulously spoiled Sharpay in the sensational movies.

'I'm looking forward to the challenge of making my celebrity dance-floor ready,' he admits. 'And I am so excited to share the dance floor with some amazing professional dancers and will hopefully be picking up a few tips from them. I'd love to have a celebrity partner who is young and fit but more importantly, I want to have fun in the training room – because that's a crucial part of learning a routine.'

Schwimmer, whose daughter also became his dance partner. In 2002, he performed with brother Joshua and sister Alexandria at the opening ceremony of the 2002 Winter Olympic Games in Salt Lake City, where

JARED MURILLO

One of seven children, the 22-year-old was born in Honolulu, and was inspired to take up dancing at an early age by his older brother and sisters. Jared began ballroom lessons at the age of six and, after moving to Utah with his family, he attended the Center Stage Performing Arts Studio in his home town of Orem. 'They gave me constant encouragement to fulfil my dreams,' he recalls and, by the age of eight, he had already performed with Donny Osmond in a production of *Joseph and the Amazing Technicolor Dreamcoat*.

After training with world-class instructors, Jared started to compete and was soon taken under the wing of legendary West Coast swing mentor Buddy

he caught the eye of Hollywood choreographer Kenny Ortega, who later cast him in *High School Musical*.

At 21, the Hawaiian hoofer became the US Open Swing Youth Champion and, despite his sojourn into musicals, he still loves to compete.

When he is not tearing up the dance floor, Jared is busy as a pop star. He is a member of the boyband V Factory, who are signed to Warner Brothers Records and released their first single, 'Love Struck', in the US in 2009.

Listing his specialities as pop, jazz and swing, Jared promises to bring 'a touch of the West Coast to the *Strictly* ballroom'.

V hunk Scott has broken hearts all over Walford since joining *EastEnders* in 2007, and the ladies in the audience will be keen to see him in those sexy salsa shirts.

Sadly, the one lady he would like to watch him dance is no longer able to. 'I decided to take part in *Strictly Come Dancing* because my nana, who passed away two months ago, would have loved knowing that I was taking part in the show,' he explains. 'She was very into ballroom dancing and

The next five years saw Scott travelling all over the world and modelling for designers such as Versace and Armani.

On the advice of Hollywood star Bill Paxton, Scott decided to try his hand at acting and studied for three years at the Guildhall School of Music and Drama. A role in the TV spin-off *Lock, Stock* in 2000 was followed by the offer of a regular part in *The Bill* as DS Hunter. His latest incarnation, as nightclub owner Jack Branning, has seen him bedding sisters Ronnie and Roxy,

used to dance with my granddad – in fact that's how they met. They basically brought me up and so I grew up watching them dance. My granddad is still here and he is so looking forward to coming to watch me!'

Despite a long stint in *The Bill* before he moved to Albert Square, the 39-year-old former model is not used to live television and recently took a lot of flak for fluffing his lines in the soap's much-hyped live episode. But he thinks he will handle the judges' criticism as well as the next contestant.

'I don't think anyone likes criticism,' he admits. 'If you do something wrong you do it wrong and you have got to try and correct it. I want to do the best I can. If something goes wrong, you can't collapse. It's how you continue that's important.

'People don't like people who apologise. Things happen and you have to lift your game. A great example of this was the 'live' episode of *EastEnders* where I totally blanked. I got a bit of criticism about it but I just needed to pick myself up, which I did.'

Scott was born in Woolwich, south-east London, and at sixteen, he joined the marines but was forced to leave after injuring his ankle. A stroke of luck launched his career as a model after photographer Bruce Weber spotted him on holiday in Miami.

his brother's wife Tanya and neighbours Sam Mitchell and Chelsea Fox before being paralysed in a shooting. For the last two years he was voted Sexiest Male at the British Soap Awards and won Best Actor this year.

But his much admired body is not the result of hours of working out, as wife Estelle and son Zac will testify.

'I want to get fit and I have not done anything like this before so it's going to be a challenge,' he says. 'When you are young and you have no responsibilities it's easy to stay fit and go to the gym, but since I have had a kid and I am working so much the gym has fallen by the wayside. People see my character Jack as this fit bloke, which is an ongoing joke in my household as it could not be further from the truth – when I come home from work I generally just collapse on the couch.'

While he may have the female audience in a flutter he admits he usually only dances 'after a few beers' and that he avoided dance lessons at college.

'I have no dance experience at all. When I was younger I went to drama school and one of my classes was show dance but I used to bunk that,' he says. 'I have never been into musical theatre, in fact, the thought of it brings me out in a nervous rash! But I have always liked the idea of learning to dance and that's what interests me about *Strictly*.

'Samantha Womack [Ronnie in *EastEnders*] has always said she thinks I would be great at musical theatre, so you never know – this might unleash my musical theatre career.'

Scott's biggest worry is memory loss, something he occasionally suffers from when tired. 'I think I have a little bit of ADD and at school I was described as a bit of a daydreamer. Generally I find it hard to focus for a long time and I don't want to be so exhausted that I can't retain information, so I'll need to organise myself properly and make sure I get enough sleep.'

With a full-time job on *EastEnders*, hours of training and a family to fit in, that might be harder than he thinks.

caustic craig

After seven series of *Strictly Come Dancing*, Craig Revel Horwood is still getting into scrapes with his fellow judges and one or two of the professionals. This year saw the usual spats with Len, who announced in one show that 'he needs a check up from the neck up'. There was also the occasional bump with Bruno and a near brawl with Brendan Cole, who stormed out after partner Jo Wood was dubbed 'a bush kangaroo'.

'I wasn't being personal,' insists the Aussie judge. 'I was talking about the dance. She was skipping about so it was what the dance reminded me of.' Ever fair with his insults, Craig doesn't mind picking on someone a bit bigger than him either. He took on the might of boxer Joe Calzaghe after his tango, when Craig commented, 'Two words: rigor mortis.'

'That comment came out of the blue,' Craig admits. 'I don't know where that came from but that's all I could think of at the time! He was just so stiff. He soon realised I was talking about the dance. I don't go on there and make stuff up, I only react to what I see.'

Despite his firm but fair stance, Craig understands that the task that lies ahead of this year's celebrities is a tough one and that to get to a professional standard in a matter of weeks is almost impossible.

'You can't possibly learn as much as the pros know in such a short space of time,' he argues. 'Three months may seem like a long time but it's nothing. A professional will work on a routine for three months to make it perfect but we are asking the celebrities to come up with ten different styles of dance in that time, sometimes in less than a week.

'What we are asking for is a professional attitude to dance, and not mucking around, because it's not a joke from our point of view. We're there to wave the dance flag and it's our job to judge the dances as fairly and as accurately and as technically as we can, and I think we do that. Obviously we have differences of opinion – Len and I don't always see eye to eye – but ballroom is what he does for a crust and I am a director and choreographer so we see things in different ways.'

ON PHIL TUFNELL'S BUTT-WIGGLING IN THE SALSA

'That elongated opening that belonged in a lascivious nightclub in Soho didn't do it for me, due to the fact that you didn't really dance after that.'

AFTER LYNDA BELLINGHAM'S TANGO

'That was the longest one minute thirty ever.'

ON ZOE LUCKER'S WALTZ

'Sickly sweet, saccharin, full of heinous sentiment for the opening part, and then when [you] started to dance it became tasteful, elegant.'

AFTER RICKY WHITTLE'S RUMBA

'Slick, confident, masculine, sexy.'

94

what did craig really think of series 7?

Who was the most consistent dancer?

Ricky Whittle was brilliant from day one. He was totally adored by just about all the women in the audience – and a fair few men. He's fabulous to look at, he can bump and grind, but he's not a technician and that was sometimes his downfall. Ali Bastian was a great technician but was often a bit cool on the dance floor. She didn't show her fun-loving personality through her dance. That's why the Viennese waltz suited her the best, because she is your classic type, and you don't have to have a vivacious personality for that dance to work.

Did the best man win?

Technically, no, Chris shouldn't have won but personality-wise, he had the audience on his side. Did he do the best dance on the night of the final? I would have to say yes. The Charleston was everything the show is about and if Ali and Brian had done the same Charleston routine, to the same music, they could have won. 'Fat Sam's Grand Slam' is such a clever choice of song and that makes a difference. Lots of factors are needed to make it work – the choreography has to be good, the talent has to be there, the music has to be enjoyable and the lead-up story has to be good, to keep people interested. It all came together for Chris and Ola in that dance.

ALI BASTIAN'S FOXTROT

'I'm very disappointed. I could not find a single thing wrong.'

ON JO WOOD'S SAMBA

'Futile and ineffectual. A complete dance disaster.'

Who was the worst dancer?

Rav Wilding was nice to look at but he couldn't dance. Joe Calzaghe was terrible. Craig Kelly had ideas above his station. He is one of the many people we come across who don't listen to the advice of the judges and obviously has more talent as an actor than he has in his two left feet. It's great to believe in yourself but you also have to stop and listen to what people are saying and take that advice on board.

Who was the biggest surprise?

My biggest surprise was Joe Calzaghe for all the wrong reasons. The weird thing is I did a plethora of interviews before we started, saying 'Joe Calzaghe will be good. As a boxer he'll be fleet and fast of foot, he must have timing and he must have good stamina.' I thought the quickstep would be his sort of dance because he's springy. How wrong I was!

Were you disappointed that Jade left?

Jade would have risked her career as an athlete had she stayed. It was such a terrible shame she was injured. She would have made the final because she was a brilliant dancer. She was also very motivated and that's what I love about the athletes.

Most surprising exit?

Zoe Lucker - over the last few years we have come to learn that if you are in the centre of the leader board you are going to be battling to stay. You need to hit either the top or the bottom in order to get the public to side with you. Zoe was in the middle – we loved her, she was a fabulous dancer and really great to have around.

Who was the best sport?

I really liked Natalie Cassidy. She often had terrible technique but she was very watchable! She threw all of herself into it and she had no inhibitions, which I thought was great.

Should the tough training drive anyone to the brink this year, help will be at hand. Clinical psychologist Pamela Stephenson can provide on-set therapy as well as a few good laughs, having been a hugely successful comedienne before studying psychology.

Born in New Zealand and raised in Sydney, she studied at Australia's National Institute of Dramatic Art, graduating in 1971. She moved to the UK after marrying actor Nicholas Ball and in 1979 shot to

did a bit of ballroom when I was about eleven and that was my first introduction to partner dancing. I used to do hip-hop and lyrical dance when I lived in LA and now in New York I try to do everything that's available, which is easy as the social dance scene is great.'

Living in Beverly Hills, she and Billy have hobnobbed with the Hollywood set and Pamela recalls a memorable night out with a screen legend.

'Robert Duvall is a huge tango fanatic and we went to a little house outside central LA with him

fame as the hilarious, sexy impressionist in the hit comedy *Not the Nine O'Clock News*, which also starred Rowan Atkinson, Mel Smith and Griff Rhys-Jones. While working on the programme she met Billy Connolly and fell in love. The couple went on to have three daughters and married in Fiji in 1989. In the early 1990s, while they were living in Los Angeles, Pamela went back to college, graduating with a PhD in clinical psychology from the California Graduate Institute (CGI) in 1996.

After opening a private practice in Beverly Hills, she treated patients with a wide range of complaints including post-traumatic stress disorder, depression, anxiety, personality disorder and substance abuse, before moving to New York last year to be closer to her daughters who were studying there.

Pamela has loved dancing since she was a child and reveals that a bout of polio led her to ballet lessons.

'My happiest moments when I was a child were when I was dancing. I had polio when I was young that, although it did not leave me disabled, was very painful. My parents, who are scientists and would not normally do this type of thing, decided to send me to ballet when I was four to strengthen my limbs. I also

where everyone was enjoying themselves and eating and at about two in the morning all the locals started tango dancing and it was the first time I saw the tango in a social context, which I loved,' she says.

'I also first danced the salsa in Galapagos about eight years ago after a bottle of tequila, and I thought it was fantastic!'

In New York, she has joined many dance classes for fitness and says she does a ballet class to rap music and a Bollywood dance class. And one of the dances introduced in series 7 is already a family favourite.

'The Lindy hop is really popular and Billy and I enjoy dancing together but we always end up arguing as he does it on a different rhythm. We also really enjoy dancing the Scottish ceilidh together.'

Despite his own outlandish fashion sense, comedian Billy is used to his wife dressing more conservatively and Pamela reckons he's in for a frock shock.

'One thing I worry about is that I am going to get so much stick from my family regarding the costumes!' she admits. 'As a psychologist I wear grey and black suits all the time so I have decided for *Strictly* that I am going to just go for it and wear the most revealing costumes ever.

'Billy has a tendency to look at me and say, "Are you actually going to go out wearing that?" He has a problem with tight clothes, and thinks everything is too tight so he is going to have a heart attack when he sees what I intend to wear!'

PLACE YOUR BETS

As the contestants for series 8 limber up for competition, the bookies are watching closely and weighing up their chances. They will be looking at age, agility and previous dancing experience before coming up with odds for each celebrity, but they don't always get it right. Before the start of series 7 they had boxer Joe Calzaghe as favourite to win at 9 to 2!

But there is more to take into account than the obvious assets of a dancer. We have cast our eye over past form to help you decide your favourite to become the next *Strictly* champ.

Sporting Chance

Being sporty can be a huge advantage. Not only are sports people fit, determined and competitive but, when it comes to bulky rugby players and burly batsmen, the fans are surprised they can dance at all. So far, five places in the final have been taken by sports personalities.

Cricketers have had more success than other sports, with Mark Ramprakash and Darren Gough both seizing the top prize. Athletes are next on the list with two finalists: Denise Lewis and Colin Jackson. In 2006 rugby player Matt Dawson also made the final but his fellow England teammate Austin Healey was knocked out just before the semi-finals in series 6.

'Chris used to be a footballer. Footballers do well on this show – remember John Barnes. Chris used to be a cricketer too, and they do very well – Mark Ramprakash, Darren Gough. Chris also used to be a presenter on *GMTV*… There the dream ends.'
BRUCE FORSYTH introduces Chris Hollins in the first show of series 7

But being sporty isn't always a shoo-in for the semis. Tennis player Martina Hengis was first to leave in series 7 and, hot on her heels, jockey Richard Dunwoody was out second.

Soap Wars

It won't matter which part of the country your celebrity hails from, unless they call Albert Square or Weatherfield home. While *Coronation Street* has never seen one of its stars in the final three, *EastEnders* boasts one winner in Jill Halfpenny, and two runners-up in Chris Parker and Matt Di Angelo. However, Phil Daniels and Gillian Taylforth bucked the trend with a double whammy when they became the first two celebs voted out in series 6.

Series 7 was the year for *Hollyoaks* hoofers, with Ricky Whittle and former denizen Ali Bastian coming second and third. Medical dramas *Holby City* and *Casualty* had limited success before the series 6 triumph of Tom Chambers.

Breakfast Battle

While *GMTV* presenters Fiona Phillips, Kate Garraway and Andrew Castle were notorious for their two left feet, *BBC Breakfast* has produced two *Strictly* champs. Newsreader Natasha Kaplinsky was the first to take away the trophy and sports reporter Chris Hollins nabbed it last year.

Coming On Too Strong

After a triumphant start to series 7, Ricky Whittle's dance partner Natalie Lowe revealed, 'I've heard in the past that people who come out firing never make the final so I need him to stay focused.' She had a point. So far the trophy has eluded every couple with the highest score for their first dance.

May I Have the First Dance?

Pay close attention to the first couple to dance in series 8. Before Rav Wilding broke the spell on series 7, the couple that opened the first show has always ended up in the final.

Perfection and Disappointment

A perfect score doesn't necessarily mean a happy ending. Series 6 couple Lisa Snowdon and Brendan Cole hold the record for the most 40s with three, but only came third in the series.

Although he is best known as an actor, Jimi always dreamt of a career in music. As a child growing up in Scarborough, Jimi wanted to be Michael Jackson and took to break-dancing as a teenager.

'I never grew up wanting to act,' he reveals. 'In fact, since I could walk my mum said I could dance. Music has always been my life.

'When I was younger I entered talent shows all the time. I used to want to be Michael Jackson and was

he starred in his first Hollywood movie, *The Guru*, with Heather Graham and Oscar-winner Marisa Tomei as his love interests. From there he went on to play opposite Leonardo di Caprio in *Blood Diamond* and appeared in films as diverse as Guy Ritchie's *RocknRolla, 2012* with John Cusack, and the BAFTA nominated *Exam*.

Despite a busy acting career, Jimi has been waiting for years to try his luck at *Strictly*.

'I have seen *Strictly* on TV and always thought I would love to do that,' he says. 'So when the

always performing "Thriller" in my garage. Between the ages of ten and fourteen I was a break-dancer, so you can say that dancing was always what I wanted to do. I can see why I got cast in things like *The Guru* because of the dancing element to it. In recent years that side of my personality has been expressed in my DJ-ing.'

After growing up in Yorkshire, with an Indian Hindu father and an Irish Catholic mother, the family relocated to Cardiff when Jimi was sixteen, where he joined a thrash metal band, but in the late eighties he fell in love with hardcore techno, travelling all over the country to attend the best raves. Even when he attended the Birmingham School of Speech and Drama, he was looking for a way out.

'I never wanted to and still don't want to be an actor,' he says. 'I tried to check out of drama school but the head teacher, who didn't even like me, said I was the one student she believed would make the big time. What did she know?'

In 1998, Jimi got his big break playing rebel son Tariq in the film of *East is East*, a role he had already made his own on stage at the Royal Court Theatre. The following year he landed a role as a young doctor in *EastEnders* and after leaving Albert Square,

opportunity came I jumped at it. All the way through my career I have always been attracted to things that have been challenging.'

Although he wants to do well in the show, he hopes he won't take the judges' criticism too seriously.

'You have to soak up as much as possible and then you are the one with the power. If you can get through the barrage of criticism and not have risen to it then you have the power. Criticism affects every person but you just need good people around you.

'I think humour is always a good way of dealing with things. I have never really taken myself that seriously, although I have never been live on TV and taken criticism so I don't know how I will handle it.'

The 37-year-old actor, who has a nine-year-old daughter called Meg, is hoping he will be able to look good on the dance floor.

'I am so looking forward to going on this journey. I have never put myself in this arena and I want to prove to myself I can do it. It's such a great opportunity to learn to dance and hopefully I will make my friends and family proud. My hopes are that this experience will take me in an exciting new direction in my life and my fears would be that I do not make a good account of myself.'

strictly

As only one lucky contestant can walk away with the glitterball at the end of the series, it's not always about winning but it is definitely about the taking part. Many celebrities provided moments on the show that stick in the minds of *Strictly* fans for more than their dancing ability. Our *Strictly Come Dancing* awards pay tribute to those who went that extra mile in the name of entertainment.

Bravest Performance
Laila's Rumba

The plucky actress sprained her ankle before her week nine rumba but vowed to carry on regardless. After limping on with a bandaged ankle she had to stop dancing halfway through, to be carried off by Anton. 'You're so brave,' an admiring Tess Daly told her. 'Thanks for carrying on. It was touch and go as to whether [you] would dance tonight so we really appreciate you having a go.'

Best Acrobatics
Ricky's Salsa

Ricky Whittle wowed the crowd and upset Len with an impressive backflip at the end of his week four salsa. Bruno and Craig loved it but Len scolded, 'Parts of it tickled my fancy but to be honest I'm not keen on backflips and stuff,' and Alesha called it 'corny and not cool'. There's no pleasing some people!

awards

Best Body Flash
Jade's Salsa

Jade gave the viewers an eyeful when she performed a handstand and fell out of her dress during the week four salsa. A shocked Ian covered her up saying, 'She popped out!' And Len joked, 'It was an eye opener!'

Corniest Opening
Ricky Groves' Jive

EastEnders star Ricky Groves began his week five jive by combing his hair and declaring, 'All right, you city cats. We're gonna spread a lot of jam.' His jive, to 'Boy From New York City', wasn't bad but his Big Apple accent was rotten.

Biggest Disappointment
Ricky Whittle's Thong

'If it gets me to the final, I'll dance in my thong,' joked the *Hollyoaks* hunk before starting the competition. The wardrobe ladies obligingly knocked up a sequin-studded thong with his name emblazoned on it but when push came to shove, it was decided the muscle-bound actor should shun the strip on grounds of decency. Sorry, girls, this is a family show.

Weirdest Fact

Crimewatch presenter Rav Wilding split his trousers in week one and it's hardly surprising. The diameter of one of Rav's thighs was bigger than partner Aliona's waist.

Len Goodman's Special Award

The head judge was particularly impressed with Brendan's nurturing attitude towards partner Jo Wood. After a disastrous samba in week six, he commented, 'If the Queen gives out special awards for services beyond what is expected, Brendan, you should get one because what you've done with Jo is little more than fantastic. She can't dance, you're dragging her through it and you're performing and showing Jo in the best light you can. You've given up your talent for Jo.'

By signing up to the programme, Ann has already gone down in the *Strictly Come Dancing* record books as the first politician to compete. With a reputation for speaking her mind and shouting down her opponents, the judges could be in for a real shock. And the former Conservative MP for Maidstone is not giving much away.

'Having been a politician I am very used to criticism and just tend to let it flow over me. As far as

'I would never have taken part in *Strictly* when I was a politician as it would have been seen as undignified,' she explains. 'But after seeing John Sergeant take part and seeing that you can do the show and not be able to dance I felt inspired.'

As a committed Christian Ann says she will be keeping it clean on the dance floor – so no raunchy rumbas from her.

'I will definitely prefer ballroom as I'm not

ANN WIDDECOMBE

how I will react with criticism from the judges, I will just have to wait to see what they say before I can predict how I will react!'

Ann was born in 1947 in Bath, Somerset, and began her political career as a district councillor in Runnymede. In 1987, she became an MP when she won the seat of Maidstone, which she held until standing down in the 2010 election. She rose through the ranks to various ministerial positions in the John Major government, including Minister of State at the Home Office, with responsibility for prisons and immigration, which meant she visited every single prison in the UK. She soon became a darling of the media for her forthright attitude and unstinting views, famously describing her boss, Home Office Minister Michael Howard, as having 'something of the night about him'.

In 2000, Ann turned her impressive language skills to the written word and her first novel, *The Clematis Tree*, reached number eight in the *Times* Bestseller List. After her retirement she moved from Kent to Dartmoor to concentrate on her writing, and is currently working on her fifth novel.

She was encouraged to join *Strictly* by a notorious former contestant.

interested in sexiness. I will only go at a pace I deem fit and dance in a style that seems modest. I shall make sure my dresses are of a proper length and what I would not show the Pope I shall not show the audience.'

It has been several years since Ann took to the dance floor and she is keen to learn a few new steps.

'I have absolutely no dance experience apart from when I was fifteen I learnt to ballroom dance in Guildford,' she says. 'However, I have not learnt to dance since and am really looking forward to it. The last time I danced was probably at an Oxford Comm ball, as I prefer nights in with a good detective novel.'

The formidable politician, novelist and broadcaster is going into the series to 'have some fun' and she is positive she won't begin to take it too seriously.

'I have recently had eye surgery so I will be coming into this as the least fit person, as I have not been able to go walking at all. But I am not worried about anything, as compared to what's going on in the world this is all very trivial.'

The judges should be quaking in their boots.

BEHIND THE SCENES
Putting on the Glitz

The vast selection of eyeshadows, foundations, powders and glosses required for the show

Hundreds of hairpins, ties, grips, clips and lots of hairspray fix the dancers' hair in place

Each celeb and dancer has a folder of hair and make-up ideas tailor-made for them

Standing at the top of the stairs, waiting for their dance to be announced, the competing couples are glammed up to the nines. Their make-up is perfect, the dresses are amazing and there is never a hair out of place.

Yet seconds before the camera turns on them, a small army of make-up artists, hairdressers and designers are still putting the finishing touches to their masterpieces.

'I normally have a team of five plus me,' explains make-up designer Lisa Armstrong. 'We need a team that size because, although we are not horribly busy during the day, come band calls, dress run and make-up changes we will be on set, at the side of stage, applying lip gloss, two minutes before they go onstage. Then we do all the boys, the quick changes, and then the show, which is frantic.

'When Bruce is linking back to them, we run up the stairs and the voice says, "Dancing the waltz, would you please welcome..." and that's the two seconds we have to finish off. Then the camera is on them and we have to be gone.'

Lisa is backstage at the quarter-finals, eight hours before the live performance begins, and has been talking colour tones with Ali Bastian. Spread out on the counters around her are a bewildering array of colours and brushes. For this show Lisa brings six cases of make-up, including more than 300 brushes and hundreds of shades of eyeshadow, as well as two cases of nail varnish.

As she chats, Lisa applies black smoky shades to Ali's eyes for the tango, and adds dramatic red lipstick. For her second dance, a samba, the lipstick shade will be changed to complement her dress. In a frantic day for the celebrities, the make-up room provides a welcome oasis of calm.

Lisa gives Ali sultry smoky eyes for her samba

Flavia rehearses with her hair in rollers so the curls don't fall out too soon

'This is nice,' Ali explains. 'It's kind of downtime. I can just sit, regroup, catch up with all the news and it's like the calm before the storm.'

Lisa's day begins around 9 a.m. when a few of the dancers and celebrities are already arriving. They have half an hour with the hairstylists, where they are 'prepped' for their style, then an hour in make-up, then back to hair to have their hair put in rollers or set.

comes they've been dancing and running around for twelve hours,' explains hair supervisor Laura Solari. 'We actually stitch the styles in if we do a plait or a weave or we use tiny dental bands, and then we use a big curved needle to stitch them on to the hair so there's no chance it's coming out.'

Erin in rollers with the photo that is inspiring her hairdo for the waltz

The team discuss Laila's look for her salsa

After that they go off to rehearse, usually with rollers in place, before returning to hair to have their style finished for the dress rehearsal.

'The hairstyles are finished by the afternoon but you have to keep checking them, even after the show starts, because by the time the dance off

'If it's a down style for the Latin we'll dress it out as late as we can after the dress run, or we'll do it completely from scratch. The whole thing has to be reset because they sweat and move a lot and the heat ruins the style.'

By midday, the narrow backstage corridors are awash with beautiful colours as the girls rush here and there in their full costumes and make-up and

more. Plus the skin gets sore, they get tired, and it's nice to have a little freshen up before the show.

'For the girls we can't do that because it would take too long. We do the eyes first, because all the shadow falls onto the face.'

Planning hair and make-up begins a couple of days before each show, when Lisa and Laura receive details about the final dress design. Each girl has her own folder in which Lisa records

Anton, Laila, Ricky and Natalie chat in a moment's break between dances as they wait to be called on to the dance floor

Laila gets a last-minute retouch before she heads out to the dance floor

Ola rearranges her skimpy outfit as the team put the finishing touches to her hair

Kristina's glamorous looks for the show are mapped out in her style folder.

with their hair in rollers. In stark contrast, most of the men are still in jeans and T-shirts. For them, any styling needs to be more last minute, especially when it comes to make-up.

'The boys only take about twenty minutes and they come in just before we go live,' explains Lisa. 'There's no point in doing the boys before the dress run because they're flinging the girls around and that sort of thing, so they sweat

information as well as storing essential make-up items.

'Inside are eyeliner, mascara, make-up brush and sponge, so everyone knows that they are only using their own,' reveals Lisa. 'I have a file with all the dresses they have worn through the series, plus hair and make-up, so we have a back reference and we don't double up.

'The folder has all the details of the vibe we are going to go for, including pictures of the look I have sourced elsewhere. We know the celebrities' likes and dislikes. I get the dress design, the style of dance and the music and I have the week to plan it. Then I come together with Laura on Thursday and we work together from there to finalise the look.'

As it's the quarter-finals there are only four couples left but that doesn't make it any easier. As well as

Flavia is transformed from sexy to elegant as she changes between her cha-cha-cha and American smooth

Dance partners Vincent and Flavia practise some Latin passion in the corridor

styling a whole host of professional dancers who are performing, the celebs are dancing twice, meaning a radical change of style mid-programme.

'This is the first week of two proper hairstyles,' says Laura. 'Tonight we have Ali Bastian doing a tango, so her hair has to be quite sleek and pulled back into a bun at the back. Then for her samba, we take it down so it's hanging down her back and it echoes the shape of the dress.

'After the performance she has to go back into the style of her highest dance so we may or may not have to put it back up. So including the dress run Ali's hair will be up, down, then probably up.

'I try to design styles that will work for the quick change. Today Natalie Lowe is doing the foxtrot and cha-cha-cha so she has a twist, then a side bun, then she has a third change because she's doing the MGM dance and she's having a different bun for that.

'Flavia's opening with a show dance so she's got her hair dressed for the cha-cha-cha, then we've got to change into her American smooth hair for the MGM dance, then tango hair for her dance with Vincent. That's why today's show is so busy for me.

'Things can change at the last minute too. Erin was supposed to be going in with her cha-cha-cha hair at the top of the day but now we've found out she's doing the American smooth pre-recorded before the dress run.'

To make sure the dancers are all happy, Laura consults them about each style but sometimes she has to put her foot down.

'Some girls love their hair down for ballroom and it should *never* be down for ballroom, classically,' she

says. 'But because this is *Strictly*, everybody wants to be fabulously glamorous. The professional dancers can bend the rules because no one is studying the line of the neck but the celebrities are being judged.'

While Laura manages to keep the celebs happy, she doesn't always please her mum!

'Natalie loved her rock-and-roll style, with the bow made out of hair, but my mother hated it. She was a hairdresser in the sixties so she knows how to do a lot of those styles, but Natalie loved it. She looked really edgy, which is a good look for her, and more importantly she believed in it.

'That's what we try to do more than anything. If they walk out of here with the whole look and they believe in it, that's great. Because if they can't sell the look, they can't sell the dance.'

Katya shares a joke with a member of the hair and beauty team

s a teenager, legendary goalkeeper Peter Shilton was often found brushing up on his ballroom and he reckons it made him a better footballer. 'I would go down to the Palais when I was fifteen, sixteen, seventeen because that's what they did in those days,' he remembers. 'I just had the basic lessons in foxtrot and the waltz. I did it to help me with my goalkeeping, to make me a bit lighter on my feet. I kept it a secret from my teammates though!'

Strictly is not the first time Peter has tackled a dance for the delight of TV audiences. In March 2010 he and Jason Cundy performed to Will Smith's 'Men In Black' for Sport Relief, an experience that has given him added hope for the *Strictly* challenge.

'I'm quietly confident,' he says. 'Back in the day I was pretty good but I was a bit shy so I struggled. I still am a bit shy really, sometimes, but it's become better as I've got older. I did *Let's Dance for Sport Relief* recently with Jason Cundy. He's half my age! We did

By then the promising player was already training with Leicester City at schoolboy level and in May 1966, aged just sixteen, he made his debut for the club against Everton. He spent eight years there, racking up 286 appearances and gaining his first England cap in 1970, before moving on to Nottingham Forest in 1977 after a brief stint at Stoke City. He then helped the club win the First Division in 1977–78, the League Cup in 1979, the European Cup in two successive seasons in 1978–79 and 1979–80 and the European Super Cup in 1979.

His career with England spanned four managers – Alf Ramsey, Don Revie, Ron Greenwood and Bobby Robson – and earned him 125 caps. He also boasts 66 clean sheets, seventeen consecutive appearances as goalkeeper in all England's matches at the 1982, 1986 and 1990 final tournaments and captaincy of the team on fourteen occasions.

But perhaps his most memorable moment was one he'd rather forget – being on the wrong end of Diego Maradona's infamous 'Hand of God' goal, which sent England out of the 1986 World Cup.

By the time Peter hung up his goalie gloves in 1997, he had played 1,391 official games including a record-breaking 88 FA Cup appearances.

the "Men in Black" dance, all sharp stiff movements. I only had four days to learn the routine and to practise it. But we did okay! We nearly made it to the final! I was a bit nervous beforehand but as soon as we started it was fine, it felt a bit like I was walking out on to the pitch. I'm a performer, really, and I love to perform. I get a buzz when I walk out of the tunnel on to the pitch and that's how I felt then.'

As an England player for over twenty years, Peter has taken his fair share of flack but he believes that will stand him in good stead when it comes to the judges' comments.

'Being a goalkeeper you get some great moments but when it all goes wrong you do get a lot of criticism and some of it can be quite nasty,' he admits. 'I do like constructive criticism but blatant criticism annoys me. You learn to block it out.'

Although he has plenty of work as a motivational speaker Peter, who celebrated his sixtieth birthday in 2009, is thrilled to have another sporting endeavour in his life.

'It's a great show and I love watching it,' he says. 'I'm doing this partly for fun but mainly for the challenge of it. As a sportsman I am a competitive person by nature and since having stopped playing football I need to do something challenging every now and again! That's why I do after-dinner speaking. The morning after a big dinner I feel great – I feel as though I've played a game.'

And he promises that nerves won't get to him.

'I'm nervous about going out in the first round! Or falling flat on my face. I will be nervous but they will be controlled nerves. I made a mistake on *Let's Dance* with my glasses – I ended up looking like Eric Morecambe, all wonky. But I just laughed through it and kept going, and it didn't seem to affect our performance too much, we still did pretty well.'

Looks like the legendary goalie has his eye on the (glitter) ball.

STEPPING

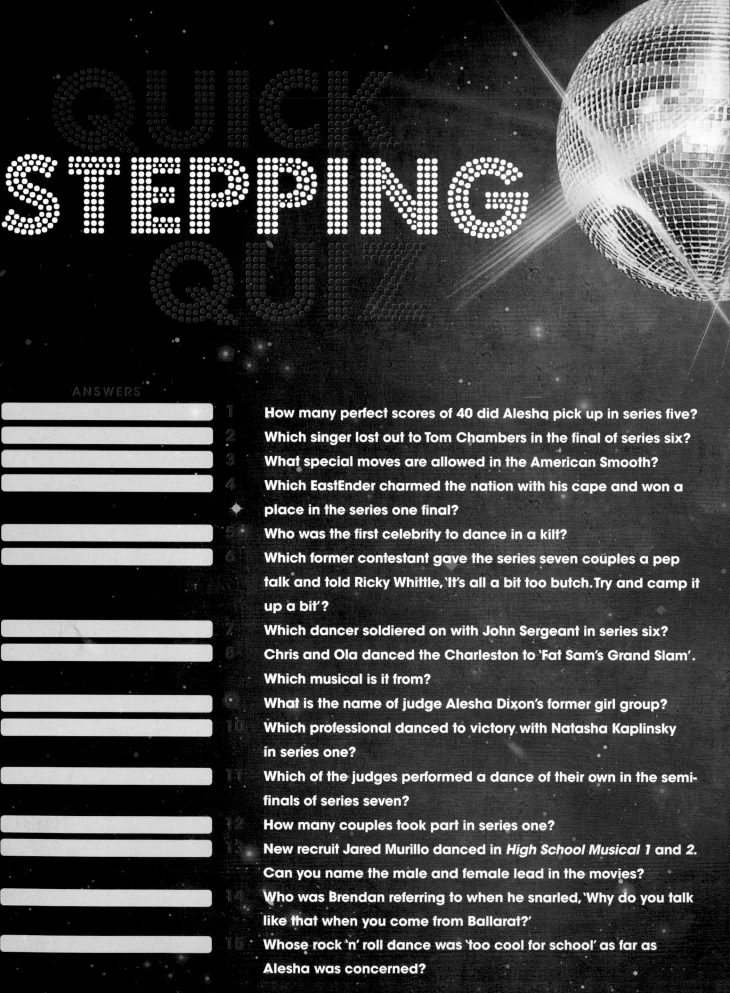

ANSWERS

1. How many perfect scores of 40 did Alesha pick up in series five?
2. Which singer lost out to Tom Chambers in the final of series six?
3. What special moves are allowed in the American Smooth?
4. Which EastEnder charmed the nation with his cape and won a place in the series one final?
5. Who was the first celebrity to dance in a kilt?
6. Which former contestant gave the series seven couples a pep talk and told Ricky Whittle, 'It's all a bit too butch. Try and camp it up a bit'?
7. Which dancer soldiered on with John Sergeant in series six?
8. Chris and Ola danced the Charleston to 'Fat Sam's Grand Slam'. Which musical is it from?
9. What is the name of judge Alesha Dixon's former girl group?
10. Which professional danced to victory with Natasha Kaplinsky in series one?
11. Which of the judges performed a dance of their own in the semi-finals of series seven?
12. How many couples took part in series one?
13. New recruit Jared Murillo danced in *High School Musical 1* and *2*. Can you name the male and female lead in the movies?
14. Who was Brendan referring to when he snarled, 'Why do you talk like that when you come from Ballarat?'
15. Whose rock 'n' roll dance was 'too cool for school' as far as Alesha was concerned?

WERE YOU SNOOZING IN THE SALSA OR WATCHING EVERY WALTZ IN THE LAST SEVEN SERIES?

TAKE OUR FUN QUIZ AND SEE HOW MUCH ATTENTION YOU WERE REALLY PAYING.

ANSWERS

15) Who holds the record for the most perfect scores in a series (not including Christmas specials)?

16) Who is the youngest ever contestant?

17) Which former EastEnders were the first two celebrities voted out of series six?

18) Who did Bruno say had 'the potential for magic' on the first programme of series seven?

19) Who conducts the orchestra on the *Strictly* show?

20) Is the tango a ballroom or Latin dance?

21) Who did Len say could be 'the most formidable couple ever' after their first dance in series seven?

22) Which country is Brian Fortuna from?

23) Jo Wood's ex-husband is in which famous rock band?

24) Which series saw the introduction of the dreaded dance off?

25) What was unusual about the series two grand final?

26) Who cooked up a storm with Camilla Dallerup in series three?

27) Why did Bruce miss a live show, for the first time ever, last year?

28) Series one and two saw celebs tackle the waltz, cha-cha-cha, quickstep, rumba, tango, jive, foxtrot, paso doble and samba. Which two dances were added in series three?

29) Which Spice Girl danced her way into the semi-finals of series four?

CROSSWORD

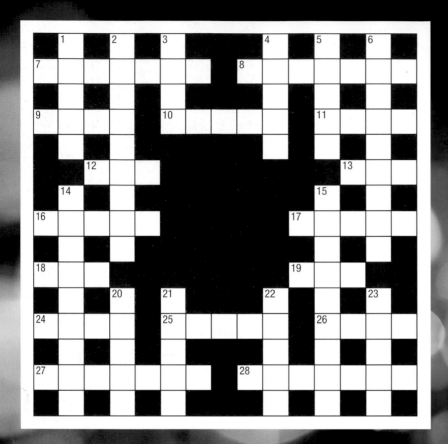

Across

7 - - - Cassidy, EastEnder who scored 34 for her foxtrot in 2009 (7)

8 & 6D Another ex-Walford star, she only made it to week 2 despite being partnered with 21D (7,9)

9 & 15D Series 2 winner who scored a maximum 40 in the jive (4,9)

10 Diarmuid - - -, gardener who holds the record for the lowest scores in the tango and the quickstep (5)

11 See 28A

12 The - - - Show, early evening magazine show formerly hosted by *Strictly* contestant Christine Bleakley (3)

13 - - - Chambers, popular winner of series 6 with Camilla (3)

16 Name shared by 2009 contestants Messrs Whittle and Groves (5)

17 See 18A

18 & 17A Dancer who gets to partner the taller celebs such as Jodie Kidd and Zoe Ball (3,5)

19 Dance - - -, system in which the dancers with the lowest overall scores perform again to avoid elimination (3)

24 - - - Johnson, long jumper whose impressive progress in 2009 came to an early end due to injury (4)

25 - - - Lythgoe, *So You Think You Can Dance* creator who was

Down

1 - - - Dickinson, antiques expert who partnered Camilla in the first series (5)

2 Natasha - - -, newsreader who was the first ever *Strictly* champion (9)

3 Claire - - -, soap actress who made it to week 8 with 28A (4)

4 - - - Phillips, former *GMTV* presenter who still holds the record for lowest ever scores in four dances (5)

5 Roger - - -, series 2 contestant who put his dancing shoes back on for Sport Relief in 2008 (5)

6 See 8A

14 Soul singer and presenter who only made it to week 2 in 2006 with 17A (4,5)

15 See 9A

20 - - - Brook, presenter and model who withdrew from 2007's competition following a family bereavement (5)

21 - - - Du Beke, popular dancer who's yet to win the competition (5)

22 Julian - - -, risqué comedian who danced with 26A in series 2 (5)

23 Climax of the competition when the remaining two or three couples compete to be champion (5)

JUDGES' WORDSEARCH

```
P C E G T E C H N I Q U E H C
N A N E V E S S O T S C C H A
S N D A R C E Y A I O R O D A
D S A I N E M R S M A R V N I
C A R M F E T M M I E I M E E
I E N N D F E E G O C S F T A
P M L C I O N N G E I L C T I
E T O L E T O R E C F D U C S
S S P N S O A G I L O I R E S
I E T P U P F T N A R S A F K
A T S E H R I F N E P A R R R
R E T Y P R B E E R L S L E A
P N Y L C S O N E E G T T P M
O E L T E E E D A H S E L A S
P T E E C N A M R O F R E P F
```

ADVICE	LEN GOODMAN
ALESHA	LIFT
ARLENE	MARKS
BRUNO	PERFECT TEN
CHOREOGRAPHY	PERFORMANCE
COMMENTS	PRAISE
CRAIG	"SEVEN"
CRITICISM	STEPS
DANCE OFF	STYLE
DARCEY	TECHNIQUE
"DISASTER"	

CELEBRITY CIRCLE

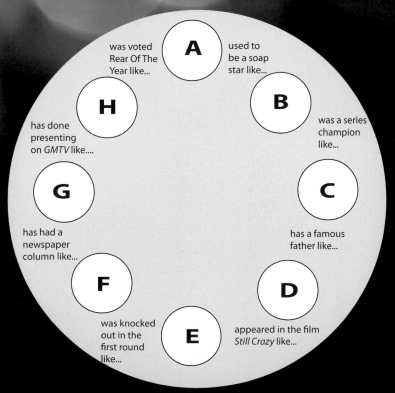

- A: used to be a soap star like...
- B: was a series champion like...
- C: has a famous father like...
- D: appeared in the film *Still Crazy* like...
- E: was knocked out in the first round like...
- F:
- G: has had a newspaper column like...
- H: has done presenting on *GMTV* like....
- (top left, near A): was voted Rear Of The Year like...

Each of the celebs has something in common with two of the others. Can you work out which fact links which celebrities and put all the people in the right place?

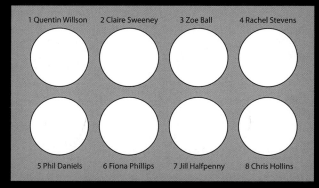

1 Quentin Willson 2 Claire Sweeney 3 Zoe Ball 4 Rachel Stevens

5 Phil Daniels 6 Fiona Phillips 7 Jill Halfpenny 8 Chris Hollins

Hollyoaks hunk Ricky Whittle burst on to *Strictly* with a waltz and a rumba that scored an impressive 33 and 32 and had him marked out for glory from the outset. Bruno called his elegant waltz 'a dream come true. The most stunning debut from anyone we've ever had' and Len awarded his first 9 of the series to Ricky's very first dance. Even the group mambo, in the first week, had two judges singling him out, with Alesha calling him 'sexy' and Len joking, 'One of the problems I've had all my life is having to perform with a muscular body, so I'm going to go for Ricky.'

Raunchy Ricky

Throughout the weeks, the soap star maintained and improved upon the incredibly high standard he and partner Natalie Lowe had set for themselves. After being knocked off the top spot in week four, they fought back with a breathtaking Viennese waltz, which earned them the first 10 of the series and from that moment on the only contenders jostling for their place at the top of the leader board were Ali and Brian. In fact, at the final count, taking into account the dances scored by five judges, Ricky had bagged an incredible average score of 40.3!

But while Ricky was grabbing the scores, Chris Hollins was growing in confidence and planting himself firmly in the heart of the nation. Looking back, Ricky realises he may have missed out on the trophy because his initial dances were so strong, but he wouldn't have done it any other way.

'There was no injustice,' he insists. 'Chris did well and it's an entertainment show. He progressed so much. I progressed too, but people don't see that because I had good marks from the off. We kicked off week one with a nine, but that's what we wanted.

I didn't want to come out and not give it my all because my worst fear was going out in the first show. We wanted to absolutely cane it because I'm not Joe Calzaghe, I didn't have that sort of popularity, so the only way I was going to get any support, and get people behind us, was to put out a performance which inspired people to vote.

'Natalie came up with some amazing choreography and luckily we were able to pull it off on our first night.'

Aussie dancer Natalie Lowe could hardly believe her luck when she first met her new dance partner.

'I could see instantly that he had rhythm,' she says. 'He showed me a few moves on the first day which made me think, "Wow, I think I've got a good one here."

But even the likes of Ricky can't claim perfection without a little work, and Natalie had to work on his posture and his pigeon toes, which Craig frequently commented on.

'Natalie had to break me down completely,' exclaims Ricky. 'She said that I had a natural rhythm

but she had to get that out of me because my natural rhythm wasn't working with her dancing technique! I used to call her "prop girl" because she had broomsticks for my posture, rubber bands to tie my knees together and all sorts of tricks.

'My posture was awful, I slouched a lot. If there is one thing this show has done it's that my posture, my stance and my frame are all much better than they were.'

While many of his fellow contestants concentrated solely on their heel turns and kick-ball changes, Ricky's workload on the soap had increased and he had to be content with rehearsing late in the evening and at weekends. But the toned trooper set his eye on the trophy and carried on. 'I only join competitions to try to win. My dad always drummed into us that we had to give it one hundred per cent, otherwise why bother turning up?'

On the night of the final, unbeknownst to the viewers, Ricky almost didn't make it on to the dance floor.

'I had a terrible back spasm in rehearsal and if it wasn't for the physio working absolute magic I couldn't have continued,' he reveals. 'It wasn't shown on the show because I wanted to be judged on whatever dance we did, but I was in absolute agony to the point where I couldn't even stand up, never mind do the moves.

'It got to me in one of the moves in the Lindy hop, which Craig pulled us up on, when I had to spin Natalie around my head and it really tore up my back. I was in agony and I was thinking, "Oh my God, the show dance has got about eight lifts!" I didn't think I was going to get through it.

'When I wasn't on the dance floor I went straight into the physio room where they tried to loosen me up and keep the muscles warm so I could get through the night. For me it was a massive bonus to be able to perform and I'd sooner break down on the dance floor than break down in the dressing room, so at least you know I gave it a try.'

Despite a closely run final, which left Ricky four points ahead of Chris but losing out in the public vote, Ricky doesn't feel cheated.

'I came away with the most points,' he reasons. 'That was really important to me and Nat, because that proved we were the best dancers and there's nothing more she could have done. Natalie came out with some amazing routines and we went out there and performed to the best of our ability and came away with a top score. Chris walked away a worthy champion with the trophy but we walked away with the title of best dancers.

'The only regret I had was that I didn't win it for Nat. From day one I said, "Her dancing is a ten, her teaching is a ten and her choreography is a ten, so the only thing that can let her down is me." That's the only negative thing I took away, I felt I had let Nat down. Natalie got into my head – she was so clever at teaching me how to do things. She was like a little Yoda, she'd trick me into performing the move so I'd think, "Wow, how did I do that?". For me, Natalie is the best dancer, choreographer, teacher to ever appear on that show.

Natalie on Ricky

'I hit the jackpot when I met Ricky. I couldn't stop smiling. Ricky is fantastic. People assume that we don't struggle, but we do struggle. To train your body to do the complete opposite of what it usually does is tough but it's the dedication and determination of Ricky, to get perfection, that makes him so fantastic in my eyes.

'He's the best dance partner I could ever ask for. We've come so far and he is a dream come true for me.'

Ricky on his favourite dance

'My favourite was the Argentine tango in the semi-final. For me that was the best night of the whole competition. I thought we were going out, we'd had a lot of problems, I'd not had as much training time as everyone else and it was all getting on top of us a little bit. That was the one dance I'd always wanted to do before the show started and it was a massive honour to perform it on the show. My dad turned up out of the blue, I didn't know he was going to be there, and we got the standing ovation for it. It is a beautiful, sexy, passionate, intense dance and I think we got the highest ever score for the Argentine tango, which is good going when you consider Mark Ramprakash with Karen Hardy, Vincent and Rachel. It's quite an honour to have that sort of achievement as well as it being my favourite dance ever.'

Ricky on his worst dance

'I loved every dance but the jive really did injure me, so Natalie had to put in a lot of pauses because my hamstrings were about to go. Craig pulled her up on the choreography, saying there was a lot of stopping and starting, but that was Natalie trying to save me from pulling a hamstring. They introduced it as the fastest jive seen on the show and it really was. I was absolutely shattered; I had nothing left in my locker after rehearsing that. My body started to deteriorate at that point. It was so tough, and hats off to Nat. She was really considerate about how my body was reacting to certain dances and she pushed me when she thought I could go further and if she thought I was about to break she pulled back a bit.'

As the series 7 coach neared Tower Ballroom, Blackpool-boy Craig Kelly excitedly acted as tour guide

Series 7 saw the long-awaited return to the home of ballroom. For logistical reasons, the show had not been broadcast from the Tower Ballroom since the grand final of series 2, when jiving Jill Halfpenny triumphed.

Head judge Len Goodman has competed on the famous floor many times in his youth and also appeared on *Come Dancing*, which was shot there. And he couldn't have been happier to be back, despite the lack of dressing rooms for the judges.

'For a dancer, Blackpool is the equivalent of Wembley to a footballer or Wimbledon to a tennis player, so of course it's lovely to be there,' he says. 'And where you get five hundred people on the show, you have a thousand in Blackpool so the atmosphere is much more electric.

'The logistics of actually doing it there are a nightmare. We had a bus parked out the back where we changed, but for the show it was great.'

The move to the northern venue was a challenge for the lighting and camera team. As the ballroom is raised, everything had to be humped up the stairs and it took twelve men just to lift the technocrane (the long metal arm with a camera on the end).

Lighting director Mark Kenyon and his team had to lug lighting rigs and cables up the stairs to set up the right ambience for the show and the set designers had to break everything up because the door to the ballroom is too small. The stunning venue does have some advantages though.

'The great thing about Blackpool is that most of the ballroom can be used exactly as it is,' explains production designer Patrick Doherty. 'So we took up elements like Tess's area, the judges' position and some drapes to mimic what we have in the studio, then we utilised their staircases in the main entrance area.

'We had to chop everything up because the entrance doors are tiny, so the judges' platform had to be rebuilt to get it in and we had to build a new area for Tess because the one from London wouldn't fit.

The sheer scale and grandeur of the ballroom left dancers and celebs alike in awe

BLACKPOOL

The Strictly pros kicked off the Blackpool show with a stunning waltz around the ascending crystal chandeliers

'This year will be interesting because Tess's area has moved position, so if we want to replicate what we have on the main show up there, we'll have to build two staircases downstage.'

For one series 7 contestant, staying in long enough to get to Blackpool was the most important goal. *Corrie* star Craig Kelly revealed, 'I desperately want to get to Blackpool – it's a stone's throw from where I was brought up. That to me would be like being in the final.' Desperate to dance in his hometown where his family could come en masse to watch, he begged the audience to keep him in and they obliged. Sue Kelly, Craig's mum, was delighted and admitted, 'Words can't explain how I feel that he's made it to Blackpool and we're all going to be there and everyone will be rooting for him and cheering him. When I used to go there in the sixties, not in a million years did I imagine I would see Craig dancing there, in the Tower Ballroom. My chest will be bursting with pride. I'm a very proud mum.'

An equally excited Craig said, 'I can't believe I made it. I'm going to go out there like this is my last dance, I'm going to give my best performance and I'm going to love it.' Sadly Blackpool was Craig's last stop and he was voted out.

Built in 1899, the Tower Ballroom has been the home of the national ballroom championships ever since. The hallowed dance floor is almost twice the size of the *Strictly* version, measuring 36.5 metres square, and the show's audience also doubles for the event.

Craig Revel Horwood was thrilled to be back after a five-year break.

'I'm glad we went back to Blackpool because I was campaigning for it,' he admits. 'It is the home of ballroom dancing and the ballroom is so grand, you could never emulate that sort of feeling in the studio. You know that hundreds of years of delicious dancing has taken place there and it's so grand and opulent. It's a wonderful atmosphere and I love it. I hope Blackpool loved it too.'

Tower Ballroom with the Strictly set in place

ormer Destiny's Child star Michelle is ready to work hard for her goal and is aiming high from the word go.

'I am hoping to achieve more dance education and also a boost in confidence,' she says. 'I totally respect what professional dancers do as it's so hard work. But I want to make sure we get nothing less than an eight!

'I know it's going to be a lot of hard work. I am a girl that likes rehearsal and the reward is the

album under her belt and after a less successful second album she released a more dance-orientated CD in 2008.

More recently, Michelle has played Roxie Hart in the West End production of *Chicago*, transferring the role to Broadway in February 2010. Although she is used to performing, Michelle keeps her dance moves for the stage.

'When I go out, I don't really dance as I feel that people are always watching me, expecting me to

performance. I would love to win… I want to win.'

Illinois-born Michelle started singing at an early age, joining the gospel choir at the church where her Pentecostal family worshipped. After high school, where she entered the Creative and Performing Arts programme, she began studying for a degree in criminology but left early to pursue a musical career, becoming a backing singer for R&B star Monica. In 2000, Destiny's Child duo Beyoncé and Kelly Rowland were looking for a new singer to replace two departing members and a friend recommended Michelle.

Shortly after she joined the band released 'Independent Woman Part 1', the theme to the 2000 film *Charlie's Angels*. The single topped the US singles charts for 11 consecutive weeks and the band rocketed to fame. They followed this with a second hit, 'Bootylicious', and their third album, and first for Michelle, *Survivor*. It entered the US album charts at No. 1 and sold over ten million copies worldwide. The band were also awarded three Grammy awards in their five years as a trio.

Destiny's Child announced their split in 2005 and Michelle concentrated on her burgeoning solo career. She already had a No. 1 gospel

bust out the latest moves,' she explains. 'When I was in *Chicago* I did eight shows a week so I did loads of dancing then.

'I would not have been able to do what I do for the last ten years without dancing but I wouldn't say I am the best.'

Michelle is no stranger to the *Strictly* set, having performed as a guest in the past, and it was this which encouraged her to take part.

'It's going to be hard but the reason I signed up is to have some fun. I performed a solo on *Strictly* in 2004 and it was so fun to be a guest, so I can only imagine its going to be even more fun to be contestant."

The 30-year-old singer is 'looking forward to the attitude and fun in the Latin. The jive looks like it takes your breath away.'

And she is prepared to work hard to impress the judges and the public each week.

'I am my own worst critic and I am nervous as I want to exceed expectations. I am also worried about being judged. This is a chance for people to see me as they have never seen me before and I am really looking forward to that.'

Watch out for some bootylicious booty shaking from the sassy star.

BEHIND THE SCENES
The Show

Ali grabs a last chance to practise in her costume, and test the movement of the heavy layered skirt

Waiting for their cue, Anton and Laila stand in the wings before their American smooth

In a moment of quiet before the storm, Anton takes in the view from the top of that famous staircase

As show time approaches, excited audience members gather in a canteen on the BBC complex. The room is full of beaming faces and animated chatter and a quick glance around the room confirms that the audience has dressed for the occasion, with almost as much glitter and sparkle on display as the backstage wardrobe department.

'My little girl is really excited because she thinks I'm going to be "in the telly" tonight,' says *Strictly* devotee Karen. 'She asked me how I was going to get

in there. I've watched the show since the first series and I love it. For me, Ali and Brian should win.'

David and partner Carrie have travelled from the Isle of Wight to watch the show live and they're rooting for Chris and Ola. 'We've been applying for four years so we are very lucky to get these tickets this year. We had a very early start this morning, but it's very special.'

Teachers Linda and Lesley have been huge fans since the first series. 'On Monday morning our staffroom chats are all about Saturday's *Strictly*,' says Lesley. 'All our colleagues are jealous we are going tonight.'

'We want to see Ricky,' blushes Linda. 'I think he's quite mesmerising. We love the show-stopping number he did a couple of weeks ago. He's hot!'

It's 5 p.m. and backstage Ali is still having hair extensions put in while Aliona's flame-red hair is being curled for the professional cha-cha-cha. The wardrobe department is making last-minute adjustments to dresses and the rest of the celebrity

122

dancers are in their dressing rooms, changing and grabbing a snack before the main event.

With her hair finally finished just after 6 p.m., Ali emerges in her stunning tango dress and twirls around the Star Bar, a large room used for quick changes during the show. 'It feels quite heavy,' she says about her fabulous outfit. 'It's quite full.'

Sitting backstage in a classic black suit and white tie, Ricky Whittle looks dapper and surprisingly relaxed. 'I'm a chilled-out person,' he explains. 'That's the way I've been raised. My dad's very relaxed as well, even though he's in the military. He's always raised me to be bigger and better and by now I've already done all the hard work, in the training room.

'Come show time Natalie has drilled me through the routines so much that I can just enjoy Saturday night. People keep asking me if I'm scared to be in

A quick change for Chris from waltz to samba

the dance off. No, I don't care about the dance off because if you get scared in the dance off, you're going to freeze up, forget stuff or try too hard. You have to embrace it as an opportunity to show what you've got. It may be the last dance so go out there and smash it. I don't want to leave because I froze up or got nervous, I just want to enjoy it.'

Natalie is not quite as relaxed as her partner, and she's worried that his full-time filming on *Hollyoaks* has left them under-rehearsed.

'I have three dances tonight, which is crazy,' she says. 'But if we make it to the final I have five with Ricky and then pro dances on top. We are rehearsing

as much as we can but he is working really long hours in *Hollyoaks* and I don't get him until 8.30 at night.

'Even so, he's very focused today and he's done an amazing job for the hours he gets. He really surprises me.'

For his part Anton Du Beke, who is waiting for Laila in the corridor, is just surprised he's still in the series. 'It's quite nice to be dancing in December,' jokes the oft-ousted dancer. 'That makes a huge difference. I've never done that before.

'We have two dances to do so we are doing a lot of training. You just get up in the morning and go to the studio, then you go home, have supper and go to bed. But the live show, it does focus the mind.'

Five minutes before the show begins, the audience is in the studio, the atmosphere is building up and Bruce is getting the fans in the mood with a warm-up routine. Stylist Laura, who is still fiddling with Ali's hair, tells her, 'I hope you don't score highest for your first dance. I don't want to have to put it up again.' A frantic runner is rushing around saying,

Relief and excitement after another sensational dance – this time a waltz

'We're missing Anton. Everyone look for Anton,' as the other celebrities gather in Tess's famous backstage area.

The elusive dancer found, the famous music thunders through the studio and the show begins. Ali and Brian are first on for the tango, which Alesha praises as a 'great opening to the show'. The injured actress is clearly in pain as she limps offstage and into the changing area where she disappears behind a screen to change into a slinky samba number. As soon as she emerges she sits at a tiny dressing table where she

Chris and Ola moments after finding out they are through to the semi-finals

Emotions run high as the hours of work pay off

is swamped by the hair and make-up team. Eight minutes after leaving the dance floor she has been transformed from ballroom beauty to sexy Latin lover and she is back in Tess's backstage red room.

Laila is next for the quick change. Upset after a disastrous American smooth that saw several stumbles and mistakes, she mourns, 'Still no forty! There are five judges and still no forty.' As she gets into her salsa dress, Anton is helped by dresser Billy Kimberley who has worked on the show since series 1. 'It's such a lot of fun,' he says. 'They are a nice bunch this year. I don't want any of them to go tonight.'

Chris, who has just scored 41 for his waltz but caused a row between the judges over his 'lemon-sucking' face, is soon changing for his next dance. Billy, he says, is an invaluable help in the lightning transformations. 'He's a lovely chap and such a gent.'

Ricky and Natalie burst backstage after a fantastic foxtrot, danced to the classic song 'Too Marvellous', netted them 48 points out of a possible 50. Len said simply it was 'too marvellous for words'.

'I am so relieved,' says Ricky, as Natalie is preened and restyled at the dressing table. 'After what all the judges had been saying it was hard to go out there but we got the highest score ever. Mind you, we did have an extra judge.'

Having delivered 'the best samba of the series', according to Alesha, Ali hobbles back in the Star Bar and immediately plunges her ankle into a bucket of ice, tights and all. 'I bruised the bone a couple of weeks ago and dancing today has made it flare up,' she winces. 'It's been getting worse all day and the samba is quite a bouncy dance, so it is really painful now. I hope I don't have to dance again.'

Laila's evening goes from bad to worse when she forgets the routine for her salsa and gets a kicking from the judges. 'A deflated balloon would have had more rhythm,' said Bruno. 'Sloppy and floppy.' With a score of 26, she will now have to change into her ballroom gown in case she is in the dance off. Amazingly she comes backstage smiling and answers concerned questions with a breezy, 'I'm all right.'

Straight after her samba success, Ali is in agony with her foot in ice water

'We deserved the judges' comments for the salsa but I think they were a bit harsh for the American smooth,' she says. 'I know I stumbled but so did Ali and they really came down on us like a ton of bricks. It knocks your confidence so when you go out the next time you go out completely insecure and screw it up completely. But Anton and I have got used to them being terrible to us.

'It would be a miracle if we get through but I've had a great time.'

Meanwhile, the wardrobe girls are frantically drying Ali's sodden tights with a hairdryer so she can return to the studio for the close of the first show. Still in intense pain, she is finally helped back on set by Brian.

As the first part of the show comes to an end, the dancers and celebrities head backstage to prepare for the results show and change into their dance-off outfits, just in case they are chosen. Chris recalls a near disaster in his rampant samba, laughing, 'I nearly flung Ola into the stalls! I flung her round and nearly let go!'

Ricky, dressed in a sheer black shirt slashed to the waist, is elated after wowing the lady judges into giving him 10s with a sizzling cha-cha-cha, ending up with a total score of 95 out of 100.

'We have been working on that so hard,' Ricky beams. 'I have walked my whole life with bandy legs and that's the way my body is formed, so there's nothing I can do. But my pigeon toes I can try hard to correct. There are lots of things the judges tell you and it helps. They don't want to see you fall on your face. They are there to criticise but it's constructive criticism, so you have to listen to improve.'

Partner Natalie Lowe admits it has been tough correcting the problem. 'We can only improve it as much as we can without killing the structure of his body and causing injury, but we really have worked on it – and pulled a few hamstrings in the process – and it's worth it. The judges want to see that you are trying to improve.'

The Australian professional is thrilled to have got to the quarter-finals in her first series of *Strictly* and gets quite emotional at the thought of taking the trophy home.

'Winning would be the proudest moment of my life, ever,' she says. 'I'd be disappointed for Ricky if he didn't make it all the way having come this far. It's a dream come true being here, and it would be a

Under pressure – after two low scores, Anton hopes Laila and he can avoid the dance off

huge bonus if we took the trophy home in my first series. I could crack a tear right now at the thought of it.'

Back in the studio for the results show, nerves are still running high. Ricky is miles ahead of the others with a stunning score of 95, while Laila languishes at the bottom with 59. But each couple knows, as they wait nervously for the result, that even those with perfect scores are not exempt from the dance off. Finally the moment of truth arrives, and Ali and Brian breathe a huge sigh of relief as they find out they will not have to dance again. But shock runs through the studio when Chris and Ola are also saved meaning that, despite their score, Ricky and Natalie will compete in the dance off with Laila and Anton.

Laila's American smooth is a huge improvement on her first effort but once more Ricky steals the show with his slick foxtrot, and a resigned-looking Laila faces the judges to hear the verdict.

'They were so annoyingly good,' admits Anton. 'Why couldn't they go wrong a few times! No consideration.'

With Laila out, the famous theme tune begins and her *Strictly* companions gather backstage for an emotional farewell. As the audience leaves the studio, chattering happily about the evening's events, Laila and Anton are surrounded by tearful dancers amidst a melee of hugging and hand-shaking. Sorry to leave, but happy to admit defeat, the ousted actress goes home knowing that, at the very least, she has made a whole new set of friends.

STRICTLY GLOSSARY

Don't know your 'fleckle' from your botafogo? Wondering about the difference between a kick and a flick? If the judges' comments leave you baffled, help is at hand in the form of our glittering glossary.

AMERICAN SPIN
A male dancer lets go of his partner and lets her spin on her own. Most often used in the jive.

APEL
Used throughout the paso doble, this refers to the aggressive stamp of the foot performed by the male dancer. It originates from genuine bullfights when a matador would often stamp his foot to attract the attention of a distracted bull.

BALL CHANGE
A partial weight transfer onto a foot in front followed by a step on the back foot. A kick ball change is a kick, then a ball change.

BOTAFOGO
A travelling walk with a change of direction from left to right or right to left. Often performed in a samba.

CHASSÉ
This term covers a variety of different moves which all consist of three gliding steps in which the feet are closed on the second step.

CUCARACHA
A Latin step common in the mambo, rumba and salsa. The dancer places one leg to the right or left with plenty of hip movement then closes, transfers weight and repeats on the other side.

FLECKERL (PRONOUNCED 'FLECKLE' BY OUR ESTEEMED HEAD JUDGE)
A static spin in the Viennese waltz where the leader crosses his left foot across the right for the first two pairs and then crosses behind on the third. The reverse fleckerl is the opposite steps.

KICKS AND FLICKS
A term often heard in the critiques of the jive. The kick comes from the hip while the flick comes from the knee.

NEW YORK
The couple step forward side by side in promenade position while holding hands.

PIVOTS
Continuous spins.

SAMBA ROLL
A rolling movement from the waist up. The upper body circles as you create a six-step turning group and the lower body appears to catch up.

SHADOW SAMBA ROLL
An *SCD* favourite with plenty of body contact. The male dancer is behind the female, often with both holding one arm outstretched while the man's other arm is wrapped around his partner's waist. Then the samba roll is performed in sync.

VOLTA
Another Latin step popular in the samba, this involves the crossing over of the feet as the dancer steps to the side. These can also be done on the spot and are known as spot voltas.

QUICKSTEPPING QUIZ

1 None - her highest score was 39
2 Rachel Stevens
3 Lifts
4 Chris Parker
5 Kenny Logan
6 Julian Clary
7 Kristina Rihanoff
8 Bugsy Malone
9 MisTeeq
10 Brendan Cole
11 Darcey Bussell
12 Eight
13 Zac Efron and Vanessa Hudgens
14 Craig Revel Horwood
15 Ricky Whittle's
16 Lisa Snowdon and Brendan Cole (three)
17 Louisa Lytton
18 Phil Daniels and Gillian Taylforth
19 Ali Bastian
20 Dave Arch
21 Ballroom
22 Ricky Whittle and Natalie Lowe
23 United States
24 Rolling Stones
25 Series five
26 It was broadcast from Blackpool
27 James Martin
28 He had flu
29 Viennese waltz and American Smooth
30 Emma Bunton

CROSSWORD

Across:
7 Natalie
8 Gillian
9 Jill
10 Gavin
11 Cole
12 One
13 Tom
16 Ricky
17 Ian Waite
19 Off
24 Jade
25 Nigel
26 Erin
27 Willson
28 Brendan

Down:
1 David
2 Kaplinsky
3 King
4 Fiona
5 Black
6 Taylforth
14 Mica Paris
15 Halfpenny
20 Kelly
21 Anton
22 Clary
23 Final

CELEBRITY CIRCLE

A Claire Sweeney
B Jill Halfpenny
C Chris Hollins
D Zoe Ball
E Phil Daniels
F Quentin Willson
G Fiona Phillips
H Rachel Stevens

JUDGES' WORDSEARCH

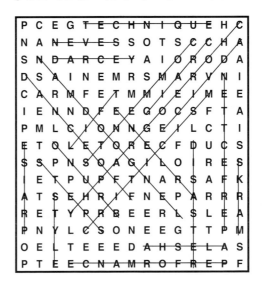

STAGE ENTERTAINMENT AND PHIL MCINTYRE ENTERTAINMENT
IN ASSOCIATION WITH BBC WORLDWIDE PRESENT

Strictly Come Dancing

THE LIVE TOUR

JANUARY

14 - 16 • **NOTTINGHAM** Trent FM Arena
17 - 18 • **SHEFFIELD** Motorpoint Arena
20 - 21 • **LONDON** Wembley Arena
22 - 23 • **LONDON** The 02
24 - 26 • **LIVERPOOL** Echo Arena
28 - 30 • **DUBLIN** The 02

FEBRUARY

1 - 3 • **BELFAST** Odyssey Arena
5 - 6 • **BIRMINGHAM** LG Arena at The NEC
8 - 9 • **MANCHESTER** Evening News Arena
10 - 13 • **GLASGOW** SECC

TICKETS ON SALE NOW!

strictlycomedancinglive.com